TRIUMPH
BOOKS

RARE GEMS

RARE GEMS: HOW FOUR GENERATIONS OF WOMEN PAVED THE WAY FOR THE WNBA

HOWARD MEGDAL

TRIUMPH
BOOKS

Triumph Books LLC
814 North Franklin Street
Chicago, Illinois 60610
(312) 337-0747
www.triumphbooks.com

Printed in U.S.A.
ISBN: 978-1-63727-198-8
Design by Nord Compo

All photographs courtesy of the author unless otherwise noted.

To Mirabelle and Juliet, my rarest gems,
and to Rachel, who makes our life together sparkle.

CONTENTS

FOREWORD

MINNESOTA, with its 10,000 lakes, snowy winters, and the iconic phrase "You betcha" is the place I call home. These are the surface-level descriptors of my favorite state, but there's so much more beneath the surface. People cherish Minnesota for deeper, more meaningful reasons: passion, strength, resilience, the spirit of fight, and an unyielding desire for change.

It's this depth that has brought me into the sisterhood of some of Minnesota's most influential and inspiring women, all of us bound together by one common thread: the love of basketball. Although our pathways and opportunities vary widely, our shared love for the game and our hunger to see it thrive unite us. From Gopher fans' favorite Peps Neuman—now affectionately known as the Blanket Lady—to pioneers who laid the foundation, such as Lindsay Whalen, to young stars like Mara Braun and Paige Bueckers, who now carry the torch, the future of our beloved sport is undoubtedly in good hands. With unforgettable performances, visionary leaders, and a true dynasty to guide those who will follow, Minnesota has found itself in the spotlight time and time again.

Today I have the honor of coaching at the University of Minnesota, where my journey began. It's a surreal feeling to see my jersey hanging in the rafters of the very gym where I once honed my skills. Now I'm passing on my knowledge and experience to up-and-coming stars, becoming a role model for them as someone who has been in their shoes. This is my way of giving back to the game that has given me so much and ensuring that Minnesota's basketball legacy continues to shine.

Yet this growth doesn't happen in isolation. It's the result of constant support and a desire to share these incredible stories with the world. It's about watching, listening, asking questions, and writing for hours—regardless of how popular or unpopular it may be—even before the age of social media excitement. It's about someone who cared deeply and understood the importance of sharing women's stories. The *someone* to whom I refer is Howard Megdal. He is one of the kindest and most passionate writers I've had the privilege to meet. Howard is a tireless advocate for the respect and recognition of women's basketball, and he's unwaveringly honest and open in his words.

Within these pages, you'll discover the exceptional lives and careers of Minnesota basketball's most influential women. Their stories are a testament to dedication, resilience, and triumph against all odds, qualities woven into the very fabric of our great state.

This book not only showcases the unwavering spirit of these incredible women but also pays homage to advocates such as Howard Megdal, who tirelessly champion women's basketball. It's a celebration of the past, a snapshot of the present, and a glimpse into the bright future that lies ahead.

Whether you're a basketball enthusiast or simply a lover of inspiring tales, this book is your invitation to a journey through the heart of Minnesota's women's basketball. Minnesota's epic winters may always be a part of its identity, but after reading this book, you'll find that it's a place that embodies so much more.

—Rachel Banham
Minnesota Golden Gophers all-time leading scorer,
assistant coach, and WNBA player

INTRODUCTION

THE GROWTH IN WOMEN'S BASKETBALL can be measured through hard-won victories large and small made despite myriad challenges. Let us gaze upon two scenes involving preternaturally talented young basketball players in Minnesota, their origin stories 60 years apart.

There is Elvera "Peps" Neuman, a 5'6" woman with boundless energy who taught herself to play the game during the 1950s, shooting on a hoop her father built for her and attached to the family barn on the Neuman farm in Eden Valley, Minnesota. In 1962 she graduated from Eden Valley–Watkins High School dreaming of a career playing professional basketball. To do it, she had to turn down an offer from her father: $100 to stay home and pursue her dreams while continuing to work on the farm.

That's what she'd done all summer after graduating, after all—that and playing on a local softball team when she wasn't busy serving meals and drinks to drive-in customers at the Root Beer Barrel. And Peps had moved on by then from her barn-side hoop to a court where she could "shoot, shoot, shoot" more than a two-mile walk from her house. She did it every chance she got, dreaming of a bigger basketball life.

She loved her life at home, though, and would have stayed if only there'd been a simple answer to this question from her father in the summer of 1962: "Can't you find basketball in Minneapolis?" Specifically, of course, he meant women's basketball, in the city just over an hour's drive from Neuman's home. The answer to his question was no.

Sixty years later, Neuman got to witness what a sold-out Target Center in downtown Minneapolis looked like on the Friday night of the 2022 Women's Final Four. Her loud cheers joined with those of the crowd—18,268 strong—to send a wall of sound toward Paige Bueckers and her Connecticut teammates. The 5'11" Bueckers may have worn her ponytail a little different than Neuman, but Neuman certainly saw herself in Bueckers all the same.

Bueckers grew up even closer to Minneapolis than Neuman had, just outside the city limits in Hopkins. A familiar sight around Hopkins was Bueckers—dressed in sweatpants, sneakers, a hat, and a hoodie—dribbling everywhere she went. Now—back home after an Elite Eight performance unlike virtually any in the history of the game sent her home to keep on playing—Bueckers looked up at the crowd, her crowd, and half smiled, her teammate Azzi Fudd's arm around her, in the huddle receiving final instructions from UConn head coach Geno Auriemma. Women's basketball was thriving in Minneapolis, as it was in so many other places.

Rare Gems is the story of how four generations of women, whose paths kept intertwining with one another's, and with the state of Minnesota itself, built so much of the infrastructure for the game of women's basketball—not just so that an individual young woman, smitten with the sounds and the rhythms of it all, could dribble by herself but so every woman in America could enjoy what, for men, had been a birthright for more than a century: to pursue greatness on the court until the day she decided to stop.

What that means for the women who play the game, of course, extends well beyond a court measuring 94 by 50 feet. It is nothing less than the challenge of building a sporting, financial, and emotional infrastructure that can welcome all who seek it. Four generations of women: Peps Neuman and her closest friend and collaborator of a half century, Vicky Nelson; Cheryl Reeve and her wife, Carley Knox; Lindsay Whalen, Maya Moore, Seimone Augustus, Sylvia Fowles, and the greatest team in WNBA history, the Minnesota Lynx; Minnesota's own Rachel Banham establishing herself as an WNBA player; and the future of the game itself in Paige Bueckers, Mara Braun, and the Minnesota professional stars of tomorrow. They have all built this thing together.

They have pushed forward into the headwinds of man-made obstacles, lack of opportunity and funding and even legality for women to excel in a game that they played virtually as soon as men did, finding an audience for it right away as well, yet being stymied by the same race- and sex-based discriminatory forces that create gaps everywhere in our society.

To do this has required an effort that is exhausting simply to catalog, let alone to accomplish. It is the story of forcing open doors—to ensure teams even existed, to allow those teams to play in conditions resembling the ones men could take for granted, to ensure that the color of your skin or who you love would not be a barrier to building a life centered around the game of basketball. To end the absurd double standard that treats every undeniable success by women as a one-off but every setback as a referendum. And then to do it, again and again, for 60 years. And still the fight continues.

That it was these women who came to lead the fight isn't a function of their desire to do battle. Some, such as Knox and Augustus and Braun, are eager warriors. Others, including Neuman and Reeve, simply concluded there was no other path but to fight. All of them have won victories that have reverberated for generations, and will continue to do so, and that has set 21st-century women's basketball on a course that wouldn't have been possible but for them.

This course has not been a straight line. The triumphs have not always been straightforward. Every moment within the progression of women's basketball, it is possible to simultaneously marvel at the distance traveled and to look wearily ahead, frustrated at what is still left to accomplish.

And so it has helped too that all of these women, from Neuman and Nelson to Bueckers and Braun, have collaborated on part of their journeys together, to extend ladders of opportunity down, to reach across generations to share wisdom accrued from similar fights, to sympathize with the frustration from the same barriers, to marvel collectively as many of those barriers have fallen, to see that even when individual goals they've held don't come to pass, the larger world they've created expands in ways almost impossible for them to comprehend.

PROLOGUE:
BEFORE THE BEGINNING

TO UNDERSTAND THE GAP between men's and women's basketball—in audience, in media coverage, and most critically in opportunity—it is vital to process it in terms of how it happened, to know that basketball, like so many other areas of American life, evolved over the course of the 20th century subject to the same fights and arguments as the women's movement writ large.

In the case of basketball, it is necessary to recognize that when it started, no gap existed, that it took frantic efforts on the part of bad-faith actors to create that gap—often under the auspices of protecting women—and then that gap has been nursed through the subsequent decades by easily debunked claims that it was, in fact, the natural order of things.

It is generally known that James A. Naismith invented the game of basketball in Springfield, Massachusetts, in 1891. By 1893 both

Geneva College and Vanderbilt University were playing men's basketball games, with each school laying claim to having hosted the first contest. That same year, Smith College put on a well-received game of basketball between its sophomore women and freshmen women, the sophomores prevailing 5–4 in a game with two 15-minute halves. (Neither men nor women had yet availed themselves of a shot clock.) "The running track of the gymnasium was crowded with spectators, and gay with the colors of the two classes," according to a newspaper account at the time. "One side was occupied by sophomores and seniors, the other by juniors and freshmen, and a lively rivalry between the two parties was maintained throughout the contest."

Senda Berenson, a future Basketball Hall of Famer, adapted the rules for women. The appetite for the game was clear. In 1896 the first game with five-man lineups occurred in men's basketball, with the University of Chicago defeating the University of Iowa 15–12 with 500 people watching. Less than three months later, a similar breakthrough came in women's basketball when Stanford faced Cal at San Francisco's Page Street Armory on April 4, 1896. There were 700 people in attendance—only women were allowed, with the broad understanding that men would prove problematic if they observed. (They tried anyway, climbing onto the roof and looking in through windows; they were reportedly batted away with sticks by women inside the building.) Stanford's Agnes Morley hit the game-winning shot. Women's basketball was outdrawing the men's game.

What happened next cannot be a surprise to anyone even remotely versed in the ebb and flow of the feminist movement. That same year, California decided not to give women the right to vote (a right they would not receive until 1911). And three short years later, in

December 1899, Stanford banned all women's athletics, asserting reasons including that it was "for the good of the students' health" and to avoid "the unpleasant publicity accompanying the contests."

Contrary to popular myth, though, women's basketball didn't disappear at Stanford. As ever in women's sports, the athletes and the ambition remained as strong as ever. All that changed—all that ever changes—is how visible it was, how many women were given the opportunity to participate, how easily opponents who either accepted patriarchal terms or were hoping to create them anew could drag society back into the bog of misogyny.

So the Stanford women simply formed a team without the Cardinals name—the Palo Alto Club—and went on playing in the proto-Pac-12 against Cal, Nevada, and Mills College. That this was so obviously the Stanford women's basketball team was clear in the press clippings that followed, wherein the team was usually referred to as Stanford.

And the rivalry was fierce! Just consider how the 1905 season ended between the two schools, after splitting two contests, according to the May 8, 1905, edition of the *Berkeley Gazette*:

> The Stanford basket-ball women are wrought up over the story to the effect that they had lost the championship to their Berkeley Rivals by default. . . .
>
> And all of the trouble arose over a selection of a date for the deciding game. Miss Jane Spalding, captain of the Stanford team, says that Berkeley asked to be excused from playing the final contest on account of the final examinations, which began at the State University last week. This information was brought to Stanford early in the week, and

considering that the season was at an end, the squad was disbanded. Late in the week a letter was received from California signifying the desire of the blue and gold aggregation to settle the vexed question of basketball supremacy by a game to be played at the end of the week. The Stanford team declined to accept this late challenge, but they absolutely refuse to concede that they have lost the series by default.

As ever, this story of women's sports involved massive pushback. The Stanford women, as well as the Cal women, were denied varsity letters for their accomplishments. Even playing sports of any kind for Cal required an artificial barrier, as scholar Kristen Wilson details in her paper "A Place for Women: University Gymnasiums, 1867–1969": "When the Berkeley women first approached a university gymnastics instructor in 1891 to ask for use of the men's gymnasium, the instructor required that they obtain physicals to prove their health, then swiftly claimed that the university did not have the funds to cover such an expense. Undeterred, the students turned to local physician Dr. Mary Bennett Ritter, who agreed to perform the physicals free of charge."

Ultimately Cal women were permitted to use the gymnasium during the men's lunch hour, and three times a week during drill hour. Since that was grossly insufficient, Patricia A. "Phoebe" Hearst, mother of William Randolph Hearst, commissioned, bought the land for, and established what came to be known as Hearst Hall, a women's-specific athletics facility, in 1900. Cal and Stanford routinely played their games there in the first years of the 20th century. Hearst Hall included a state-of-the-art basketball court, surrounded by bleachers to hold 600 spectators.

But without institutional support—and really, much worse than that, an outright ban in place—the women's game could not thrive at Stanford. (That, uh, eventually changed.) An attempt to gin up hysteria over the dangers of women's basketball could be found shortly after Hearst Hall opened, and not surprisingly, it was directed at Cal.

An alarming headline appeared in the January 28, 1900, issue of the *San Francisco Call*: PROBABLY FATAL INJURY RECEIVED AT BASKET-BALL, with the subhead, MISS MYRTLE MONTROSE MAY NOT LIVE. "During the interstate game, Miss Montrose was thrown against a post, and it was thought that only the bridge of her nose had been broken and that the injury, while painful, was not serious," the paper explains. "The injury was treated and she returned to Nevada. Since that time she has been compelled to submit to two operations, and a third is now necessary." The story goes on to explain about the many skull fragments lodged in her brain, and concludes with this dramatic and seemingly contradictory medical diagnosis: "The information from Nevada says that the young lady cannot survive a third operation, and that a third operation will be absolutely necessary." (I'd probably get a second opinion!)

A day later, the *Reno Gazette-Journal* attempted to set the record straight, under the headline FAKE STORY EXPLODED:

> Both the *Examiner* and *Call* published a fake story in regard to Miss Myrtle Montrose, one of the leading members of the University of Nevada last year's basketball team. They make it out that the slight injury Miss Montrose received while playing at Palo Alto has developed into fatal proportions. . . .

The fact is that Miss Montrose is attending the University every day, enjoys good health, has had no operations performed, and doubtless has the strength as well as the inclination to lick the man who wrote the story.

But newspaper archives reveal the fake story was reprinted countless times. The correct version appeared only once, in Reno. Montrose went on to a distinguished newspaper writing and editing career and died in 1959, from causes likely unrelated to college basketball.

But the Cal women's basketball team withered as the first decade of the 1900s continued, principally because as anti–women's sports hysteria took root at colleges around the country; they simply had no one to play. The death knell came in 1907 when Cal began a men's basketball team. The university designated the men's team as its intercollegiate basketball team. Women were left to take up the game as a club sport.

Hearst died in the influenza epidemic in 1919. Hearst Hall burned to the ground in 1922. William Randolph Hearst built what became known as Hearst Memorial Gymnasium in his mother's honor, and it opened in 1927 for women; it is still standing today. But the basketball court was not regulation size, and included no room for spectators, even as Harmon Gymnasium—now Haas Pavilion—opened in 1933 for men's basketball, contained seating for 7,000. As Wilson put it, "There was a before-Phoebe and after-Phoebe for the Berkeley women's physical education program." That is to say: even amid systematic discrimination, individuals and their work mattered significantly.

The men's game grew steadily through the early 20th century, while organizations such as the Amateur Athletic Union (in 1908) and the International Olympic Committee (in 1914) argued everything from the idea that women shouldn't be permitted to play basketball in public to one that said women shouldn't participate in the Olympics in any sport at all.

What has followed for the next century-plus is a familiar pattern. While men's sports have been watered and given sunlight at every turn, women's sports have often been ostracized by the decision-makers at what have turned out to be critical moments in the evolution of American life.

Notably, patterns can be discerned in two key ways: when women's sports make their biggest advances, that is what typically leads to a countermovement mostly directed at shutting down that momentum. The rhetoric is easy to spot—enemies of the game insist they are merely hoping to protect women, or bowing to the reality that men's sports are more popular. These tropes are visible everywhere in what's happened since, from movements against women's sports writ large to attempts to attack groups within women's sports, including LGBTQ participants and the current furor directed at the trans community from so-called defenders of women's sports who wouldn't know a WNBA basketball if it smacked them in the face.

In this way, as Carley Knox wrote in her master's of education thesis at Bowling Green State University in 2004: "For women athletes, due to the fact that being feminine and being an athlete were long considered contradictory traits for women, athleticism was often equated with a lesbian threat."

Or more simply, as Emilia Vella wrote in her senior project, "On Your Mark, Get Set, Gender! The Politicality of Women in Sports" at Bard College in 2023: "Reconceptualizing what sport is and what success looks like is how we change sports. Being set in the established systems is what intrinsically excludes those who have historically been excluded. Sports are expansive and a staple to American social and cultural life."

All of which is to say: When Peps Neuman first entered this life on October 25, 1944, the stakes for all that she'd accomplish, the slope of the mountain she and those she inspired had to climb, could scarcely have been larger or more vital. And without the life led by Neuman and those who followed, none of what women's sports have become today would be possible.

CHAPTER 1

PEPS

———

I T IS EQUALLY DIFFICULT to isolate the creation of the women's basket-ball movement—to find its progenitors, the people who instilled in women across the country the knowledge of and passion for the game—as it is the game itself. But it is particularly notable, then, who managed to find the game, grow it, and leave it a vastly more accessible place than it was.

How do we measure this? How do we account for the ebb and flow and the movement of women's basketball from isolated pockets of enthusiasm to the global game it is today? In the case of Elvera "Peps" Neuman, it requires nothing less than a full accounting of how she grew into an ambassador for the game, a combination traveling billboard for the game itself and entrepreneur who paved the way for the explosion of the business of women's basketball. And it all started with a hoop on a barn.

When Peps was born in October 1944, even amid a global world war, women still yearned for the opportunity to play basketball. The

Deseret News reported, two days before Neuman's birth, "Salt Lake City may have a women's basketball league, after a lapse of many years," with several organizations already committed to participate, from the Ft. Douglas WACs to the nurses at the University of Utah and LDS Hospital.

It was the heyday of Margaret Sexton Gleaves, who led the Nashville Vultee Aircraft AAU basketball team, the Bomberettes, to championships in both 1944 and 1945, a career that ultimately landed her in the Women's Basketball Hall of Fame. But her name was not in the one-paragraph story about that triumph in the *Minneapolis Star* on April 1, 1944, one of only five mentions about women's basketball in any newspaper in the state of Minnesota all year.

It wasn't Gleaves's story that started Peps on her journey. It was a basketball hoop her father, Emil, built and hung on the family's dairy barn. Peps was the baby of the family, and the only girl, and though her four older brothers—Clayton, Gordon, Lloyd, and Frank—all used it from time to time, she used it the most. "They were all musical," Peps recalled. "And I was all athlete. I couldn't clap my hands to music if I had to. But if I'm dribbling a basketball, I can keep much better time."

The story of Peps Neuman is unlike what girls have available to them today if they find they have an interest in the game. But her early years shaped so much of what was to come in her life. As the youngest, when she'd play pickup games with her brothers, she understood she'd need to get shots off quickly against the taller competitors. And she noticed something else too. "If I shot long shots, a lot of time, if I missed, they would bounce further back by me," Peps recalled. And with that, her early proclivity for crowd-pleasing long baskets was born.

Peps grew up working hard on the farm, combining schoolwork with chores. But she always found herself drawn to the hoop attached to the barn. Dribbling, shooting—it was all pleasure for her. The rural farm was a good three miles from the main part of town, which was only 792 people strong in the 1950 census. And at the family farm, she practiced shooting, could imagine herself dribbling around and through defenders, a skill she honed on the dirt path just outside the barn on many days after attaching the milking machine to the cows. Each cow was supposed to be milked for three minutes, but Peps would get lost in her basketball dreams, sometimes only remembering her chore after 8, 9, or 10 minutes had passed. "It was great for my game but not so great for the cows," Peps said with a laugh. "But we got more milk that way."

Those days and nights shooting at that basket hanging on the barn shaped her game in so many ways. For the rest of her life, she said she shot better in dimmer arenas, matching the farm lighting that allowed her to keep playing at night. And she never stopped playing on a miss—it was always after a final made basket when Peps, finally satisfied, went inside and went to bed.

And while there was no professional women's basketball to watch, and even the NBA was seldom on TV, it didn't matter, because Peps's family didn't have a TV for most of her childhood. Once they got one, though, in 1955, when Peps was 11, she began to be shaped by another team, one she was able to see on television: the Harlem Globetrotters.

"We used to watch the Globetrotters on TV," Peps said. "And in fact, I thought they were as good [as], if not better than, the NBA [teams]. Because they could not only play basketball and shoot all these fancy shots and do all this but entertain the people too. So maybe that's where I got it into my head that that would be great. And when I had a chance to actually join a barnstorming tour, that probably was in my mind too, that, 'Hey, we can entertain and we can play basketball.'"

Not that everyone saw it that way. Peps has a vivid memory of watching the Globetrotters one weekend and trying some of their moves the following week in gym class, particularly those of her favorite player, Meadowlark Lemon—things such as fake passes, behind-the-back passes, and putting the ball down on the floor and then coming back to get it. She said her classmates laughed, but the teacher was not amused.

By 1961 Peps knew that what she really wanted to do with her life was to play professional basketball. It was an early moment to realize her calling. It was almost inconceivable that she knew without any extant model for how to do it.

She wasn't the first woman to play professionally. Even determining who can be called the first is a fraught question. The great Ora Washington and the Philadelphia Tribune Girls dominated Black women's basketball in the 1930s. The All-American Red Heads toured the country beginning in 1936. Other teams followed, such as the Helen Stephens Olympic Co-Eds, the Grover Cleveland Alexander Stars of the World, the Ozark Hillbillies, and the Arkansas Travelers, led by Hazel Walker, who is generally acknowledged as the first woman ever to own a professional basketball team.

But Peps had never heard of those teams or those people. They weren't household names the way the Globetrotters were. Even the NBA wasn't as big: average attendance at an NBA game in 1961–62 was just 4,566, while the Globetrotters routinely drew 20,000 to 30,000 people everywhere they went, with only the size of the stadiums limiting capacity. They were the model.

And as Peps hurtled toward graduation at Eden Valley–Watkins High School, her dreams grew bigger. She'd spent most of her life believing that she would simply follow in the footsteps of her classmates and preceding generations. "I thought I'd marry a farmer and raise kids and animals, as there were no sports for women athletes," she said. Yet somehow she was able to picture a different life for herself without a model, just by piecing together what spoke to her most.

She'd heard of some high schools in Minnesota starting girls basketball club teams, though she didn't know at the time that she was fighting for something that wasn't new but, as so often has happened in women's sports, something that had succeeded and then been shut down.

Back in the 1930s, Grand Meadow High School in southern Minnesota—about three hours away from Peps's town by car—reigned supreme, posting a record of 94–0 between 1929 and 1939. Predictably, the head of the American Physical Education Association warned in 1933 that the stimulation of a cheering crowd and band, combined with the emotional and physical strain of sports, could destroy the endocrine balance in young women. It was, of course, junk science, but by 1939, with no one to play, Grand Meadow had to give up varsity basketball. The nearly 350 teams throughout the state were gone by the 1940s, replaced with intramural teams overseen by the Girls Athletic Association, or GAA.

That status quo held for more than two decades before Peps organized not only a team at Eden Valley–Watkins High School but contacted girls at other nearby schools with a revolutionary idea: why not play one another? She'd heard about a team at Grove City High School, which her cousins attended, and she obtained the bylaws they'd used to found their team and pushed for one at Eden Valley–Watkins. In her junior year, she was rejected entirely, she said, but by her senior year, the administration told her she could do it, as long as she found an advisor among the teaching staff. So she knocked on every office door but was routinely rejected—teachers were too busy; they needed to get home to their families, they said. Finally, a librarian agreed, as long as Peps and the rest of the team would practice and play when she was in the library. Other schools, which had played against Eden Valley–Watkins High School, soon followed suit. A makeshift league sprang up, all courtesy of Peps's legwork.

And so it was up to Peps to organize the games too, against places such as Grove City and Paynesville, not only getting the practice of playing but learning what it would be like to operate a team. The lack of opportunities, in this case, served Peps as a kind of internship for so much that would follow.

By March 20, 1962, Peps Neuman was resolute about what she wanted to do with her life. And so she put pen to paper in English 12 and wrote an essay titled "Yesterday Thoughts." Peps wrote, "As long as I can remember, I have wanted people to know and praise me. I want to be somebody like the first woman astronaut to land on the moon or Mars, or be famous for discovering or inventing something great.

"These are some of the reasons why I practice and practice and have taken an interest in sports. My dream and aim in life is to become a professional basketball or softball player because that is something

I love. I feel I will be famous, and that is one thing in which I have confidence."

But then Peps added this closing, a sign of what an unwilling warrior for social change she was at the time: "Although, as I think of it, I hope my aim and dream change because society doesn't approve of it."

Her teacher, Mrs. Bette Kannenberg, gave her a 92. The eight points came off for a simple reason: her teacher objected to her final line, writing, "I'll still argue about your last sentence." Peps remembered, "When she took the time to write that, she argued with me. She said, 'If you believe in something, you should pursue it.'"

But the essay laid bare an internal struggle even someone as driven as Peps Neuman would be forced to battle, the heavy lift of becoming a professional basketball player augmented further by a set of widely held beliefs that there was something wrong with wanting it. Neuman was living out the thesis being put forward at that time by Betty Friedan, whose groundbreaking book *The Feminine Mystique* was in final edits ahead of a February 1963 publication date, when it helped launch second-wave feminism, an intellectual underpinning to the calling Peps was experiencing. She did not see it this way—not at the time, not even now. "It never crossed my mind that it had anything to do with women's rights," Peps said. "It had to do with the fact that I wanted to play basketball, and that's the only avenue that I knew of."

So Peps played basketball, but in an effort to keep up appearances, she baked too—taking home the Best Homemaker Award in her senior class, something she finds amusing today. "I was trying my hardest, but I never carried that through," Peps said. "I can't cook at all."

Her high school yearbook prophecy spoke to this duality: "Elvera Neuman's basketball career has become a hindrance to her baking, as she caught herself dribbling the eggs and beating the basketball."

What she'd do instead in the kitchen was listen to her family's radio perched atop the refrigerator for reception when some of the Iowa high school girls' basketball tournaments were broadcast. To get a better listen, Peps would stand on a chair next to the fridge for hours.

But her own words? No mistaking them, nor some of the reactions to them. For instance, Peps had a school superintendent at the time who read her declaration in her yearbook—that her future profession would be "professional basketball player"—and declared it the stupidest thing he'd ever heard. Word got back to Peps, but by that point, she wasn't going to let anyone slow her down.

To help the reader fully appreciate what basketball meant to 17-year-old Peps Neuman, here are the lengths she went to, to make sure she played in a GAA-sanctioned game she'd arranged that winter: Between 8 and 10 inches of snow had fallen, and while the roads had been plowed, the Neuman family farm's long driveway "was plugged with snow," Peps said, creating a quandary for her. She continued:

> No way was a car going to make it out of our driveway. I asked Dad if I could take the John Deere tractor, and he said no, so I took my little bag and a flashlight (in case I had to walk home in the dark), trudged through the snow of our driveway, and walked the five miles of cleared highway to the game. It was around 20 degrees, and I had blotches of red on my legs. I scheduled the game, so it was my responsibility to

be there. (It would have broken my heart not to be there.)
A friend gave me a ride home. The basketball game was fun,
so it was all worth it.

There are now more than 400 high school girls' basketball programs
in the state of Minnesota, following Peps's trailblazing efforts to restore
basketball games between high schools. What's more, there has not
been a disruption to that progress since Peps's leadership changed the
GAA's rules.

During that spring of 1962 her creation of, essentially, a Minnesota
girls' basketball conference had taken her to Paynesville, where she'd
seen a professional team play—this time a group of women: the Texas
Cowgirls, owned by entrepreneur Dempsey Hovland. Peps bought a program, which included the address of Hovland's team, and contacted him
to ask for a tryout. Over Easter vacation, she left the state of Minnesota
for only the second time ever to show Hovland what she could do, in a
45-minute solo tryout in South Beloit, Illinois, just over the border from
Wisconsin. (Her only other out-of-state trip had come when she was 15:
a Farmers Union trip to Superior, Wisconsin, just over the state border.)

On a basketball court with a tile floor at the local YMCA, Peps
showed Dempsey she could run and she could dribble. Then came the
free throw shooting. Peps made 8 of 10. She was crushed. "I missed
a couple and thought, *Oh, geez, I missed my chance,*" she said. "I
[thought], *You're gonna be a pro, you better make all your layups and
all your free throws.*"

But Hovland quickly reassured her, telling her she had obvious potential and that he was impressed. A plan was formed. Peps
spent that summer of 1962 splitting time between Hovland's local

softball team near her home and working as a waitress at the local
Root Beer Barrel, marking time until the Texas Cowgirls resumed
playing that fall. With any free time beyond softball and the Root
Beer Barrel, she'd take a two-and-a-half-mile walk to the nearest
court to work on her game. Because in the fall, she'd be a professional basketball player.

She said the feelings changed around town after that, as word
spread that Peps wasn't merely dreaming of a future in the game
but that she'd secured her spot. It was the talk of Eden Valley. "As
soon as they found out I made the team, then it was all good news,
big news when I'd go to the grocery store," Peps said. "They would
kind of pat me on the back—'You're gonna go play professional
basketball! Boy, that's gonna be fun. You're traveling and doing it.
Aren't you scared?'

"And sure I was. I was a naive little girl who had never been out
of the state of Minnesota. And yeah, it was a big step for me to go
play. But at that time, I was the first one that anybody'd ever heard
of [in my town] playing professional basketball anywhere."

It wouldn't be fair to say that Emil and Anna, Peps's father and
mother, were thrilled about Peps's decision to play basketball. Anna
had gone to college to train as a teacher before marrying Emil, and
both of them felt a sense of loss—one of Peps's brothers had gotten
married that summer, and they were both experiencing what we now
call empty-nest syndrome, with their baby set to take to the road.
"Mom always helped me any way she could, though," Peps said. "But
Dad said, 'Oh, do you have to go so far? I'll give you $100 if you'll
stay home. Can't you find basketball in Minneapolis?'" The answer,
at least in 1962, was no. Not if you were a woman.

And once Peps made that clear to Emil—in a discussion that was full of sadness, not anger, from both of them—her father climbed aboard. "I guess he was fine, because he had a picture of me [in his wallet]," Peps said. "That's the first thing he'd say when he talked to people after I joined the team. 'Hey, this is my daughter. She plays basketball. She travels all over.'"

That fall, she finally crossed paths with the Harlem Globetrotters and her hero, Meadowlark Lemon. Dressed in a red sweater and black pants, Neuman took the opportunity to meet Lemon following a game the Globetrotters played in Rockford, Illinois. But she wasn't alone. "We went as a team to watch them play, and to meet him," Peps said. "And he knew we were a team of barnstormers. I was in seventh heaven."

It was a remarkable arc—to go from watching the Globetrotters and Meadowlark Lemon on television to shaking hands with him as equals just years later. But Peps did something else that night too: she watched the game closely, to see what tips she could pick up and use with the Cowgirls. Peps Neuman, you see, was just getting started.

CHAPTER 2

VICKY

V ICKY NELSON, born July 24, 1954, spent most of her childhood believing she'd been born too soon.

Like her brother Gary, six years older, Vicky grew up absolutely
basketball-mad. It began the moment she first played the game in a
gym class in fifth grade. By the time she got to high school in 1969,
Vicky had grown to 5'6" and was a strong defender and vintage shooting guard. Her friend Barb Nelson, no relation, went on to start at
guard for Concordia College. And six-foot Carol Koopman went on to
score more than 1,000 points at the University of Minnesota–Morris,
then to play for the Minnesota Fillies in the Women's Professional
Basketball League (WBL), a professional women's league that operated from 1978 to 1981. The WBL was filled with all-time great talents
such as Ann Meyers Drysdale, Althea Gwyn, Molly Bolin Kazmer, Liz
Galloway-McQuitter, and Nancy Lieberman.

Three talents at the level of this Grove City trio would have
proven formidable against any Minnesota high school team in the

13

state, despite a 1970 census population for Nelson's town of just 531. There was only one problem: Grove City High School didn't have a girls' basketball team until 1974, after Vicky graduated.

So at first, the emergence of Title IX—signed into law on June 23, 1972, and leading to, among so much else, a Grove City High School girls' basketball team after Vicky had moved on to Willmar Community College—was a complicated development for her to process. "It was kind of frustrating and probably [caused me] a little bit of jealousy also," Nelson said.

The good news for Vicky was that she had already registered on Peps's radar. And Vicky had a close-up seat to watch how Peps Neuman turned herself, and eventually her team, into a generational success story in the sport. More on that later, but first we need to again look at Peps Neuman's basketball journey to see how these two women's paths would ultimately cross.

Neuman had joined the Cowgirls in the fall of 1962, a team that was pioneering in so many ways—not only as a women's basketball team but a fully integrated one. Halftime acts were part of the show too, and anyone from Roscoe's Rodeo Roundup—whips, ropes, and trick shooting—to a man wrestling a bear to pitching exhibitions from the great baseball star Satchel Paige could be on the docket.

To play on the Cowgirls meant playing five, six games a week, often with long bus rides between games. Peps said it wasn't uncommon to follow a night game with a 500-mile trip to the next town.

Staying in touch required a great deal of work as well. Not only weren't there cell phones, Peps's farmhouse didn't get a landline until 1963 or 1964, so calling home meant calling the neighbors up the road and having one of them deliver a message. Instead, Peps became an expert letter writer, a form she prefers to this day—first to her mom, then to other friends back home and her sisters-in-law. Even this required advanced planning. The Cowgirls' home office operated out of South Beloit. So friends and relatives of the Cowgirls would send letters there, where Hovland would collect them and send the letters up ahead to whichever stop he knew was six or seven days away for the team. The night of the game, the team would tear open a manila envelope and distribute all the letters to everyone.

"I suppose sometimes I was homesick but not really, because I was happy," Peps said. "I wasn't home doing the chores or milking the cows. But I did want to know what was happening, like what was happening at church or at their farm readings or if somebody visited them or whatever. But I guess it's no different than now. It's just that we had to do it by letters."

The medical treatment paled in comparison to today as well. The floors were often unforgiving—tile was common—and Peps developed shin splints. "So what they would do, they would tape my leg from my ankle all the way up to my knee," Peps remembered. "And I think [they thought] that would hold the muscles together or whatever. And then they had me do hot, hot whirlpools. And sometimes pulling the tape off was worse than the actual shin splints."

Her team took road trips that never stopped. Even on Christmas, she and the team stayed in Michigan ahead of a December 26 date to play in Muskegon. Peps fell in with a crowd that never stopped watching soap operas. "Some of the time we would have Kool-Aid and baloney sandwiches for dinner, and I know that the girls watched *As the World Turns*," she said. "And I never knew what a soap opera really was. I'd never really watched a soap opera, and I got hooked on

As the World Turns so that when we had our portable TV, sometimes I would just stay in the van and [watch] *As The World Turns* as they went out to eat."

By the time the Cowgirls came back home to Eden Valley to play a game in November 1963, Neuman's appearance drew headline attention in the *St. Cloud Times.* The article read, in part:

> The World Famous Texas Cow Girls will play an exhibition basketball game here Thursday, Nov. 7 at 8 PM in the new Eden Valley Gymnasium. . . .
>
> The well-traveled Cow Girls have an Eden Valley girl on their team, adding luster to the attraction Thursday. She is Elvera Neuman, sometimes called the team's sparkplug guard.

Incidentally, this was around the time Neuman earned the nickname Peps, both for her energy and habit of drinking lots of Pepsi-Cola, she said.

The article went on to note the average age of the team was just 20. This was the avenue for young women who wanted to keep on playing basketball after high school. This was the talent pool for college basketball that we'd come to know in the decades to follow.

And yet while Peps quickly came to understand that this was the life for her, she also saw that there were many ways she could do it better, such as owning and operating a team herself. She quietly began enlisting help from some of the other players to make her new goal a reality.

Dempsey Hovland had turned daily operations of the team over to his wife, Florence Holder Hovland, a former Cowgirl herself, and several of the players quit over dissatisfaction with the direction of the team. Peps took a different tack. "So it was different," Peps said. "But I knew then that we were going to be forming our own team. So I put in my time, did everything right, gave 100 percent. But when fall came around, I said I would not renew my contract."

Peps was one of four partners who would own the new team, along with Linda Yearby, Bernice (then Holiday) Shafer, and Katherine Mestemaker. They called themselves the Shooting Stars. Some of the seed money for the venture came from Emil letting Peps rent out 20 acres of the Neuman family farm.

And while the lifestyle was itinerant, and the whole point remained to play basketball professionally—all while showing thousands and thousands of people all over the country the quality of women's basketball—things began to change.

For one thing, Neuman saw the effect some of the road trips had on her teammates during the Texas Cowgirls years, and she instituted limits on how far the team would travel overnight. She also quickly came to realize that the halftime shows they'd book—Roscoe's Rodeo Roundup, for example, among others—were getting a larger cut of the gate receipts. So why not incorporate the dribbling tricks she'd taught herself, inspired by Meadowlark Lemon, and be the halftime entertainment herself?

Large crowds packed into gyms in all corners of the country, watching Neuman average 30 points per game—sometimes scoring 60, 70 points in one contest—all while playing with a men's ball, by the rules of men's basketball, against men.

Then the two teams would go to their locker rooms at halftime, while Peps remained on the court. The unmistakable guitar chords from Bill Justis's "Raunchy" would play over the loudspeaker, and Peps would begin dribbling—behind her back, between her legs, on her knees, first with one ball, then two—working the crowd into a frenzy. When it was over? Back to the game.

The Shooting Stars were a hit, but change was a frequent feature of a team made up of young women in their 20s. Mestemaker had to choose between attending Michigan State—her aunt Ruth was paying her tuition and wanted her to graduate—and playing basketball. A player of Mestemaker's caliber today—a skilled five—wouldn't have to choose between the two, nor rely on Aunt Ruth for tuition. Bernice left the team, was bought out by the remaining owners, and got married. Judy Oelrich came from Royalton, Minnesota, and took over as a mainstay on the floor, 6'6" Fawn Landrum provided rim protection and rebounding, and Betty Jo Johnson hit shots from the outside. The talent was everywhere. If a girl was interested in basketball, she would usually talk to Peps after a game. Peps would try her out, talk with her, get her contact information, and go from there.

The team would almost always win—at one point, 149 wins in 151 games. Though generally Peps said they'd be treated respectfully, it was also a part of the game, particularly when a men's team was losing, that sometimes the physicality would increase. Peps didn't mind that. In fact, the only thing she didn't like was when it was too easy to win.

It was left to Peps and Linda to keep on recruiting, all while playing the game. Only the booking remained in other hands, an outfit in Pennsylvania, until the man in charge of that made a fateful error. He told Peps that in order to maximize their earnings, they needed to play up the sex appeal of the team by changing their names to the Arkansas Lassies.

Peps reluctantly went along with it temporarily. But she also knew she'd need to chart a path of her own once again. "That just made me sick, because at the time, the way people thought about it was Lassie the dog," Peps said. "Not even Lassie being a woman. But they said . . . Shooting Stars was not feminine. You needed something in your game [that was] feminine. So that's why we either had to change our name to the Arkansas Lassies or he wouldn't be booking for us. Well, we needed a booking agent."

It gnawed at her, though. She knew this was the life for her. But she wondered, on these long bus rides, just what that life should look like. There was no model. "We had to do what we had to do," Peps said. "Whether it was traveling more, or taking less money. But that's one thing I knew: the direction I wanted. I knew I wasn't going to settle for going back home and being a secretary. . . . I had only one path, and it was the one in front of me, which was to do whatever I had to do [to keep playing basketball], except . . . nothing illegal."

So beginning in 1971, Peps began running a concession on the Minnesota summer carnival circuit. It took until 1973 before Peps had saved up enough money to carry on a team all by herself and operate booking as well. Linda stayed with the Lassies, but Peps started the Arkansas Gems. At the age of 29, Peps Neuman was the sole owner, operator, booking agent, halftime show, and playmaking guard on her professional team for three consecutive seasons.

Summers meant a return to Eden Valley, the Neuman family farm, and it was a home for her team too. Peps Sports, Incorporated—the business which oversaw the team—operated out of Eden Valley, with training camp for the Gems held at Eden Valley's high school gym every summer before the team embarked on its journey of thousands of miles across the country playing ball. That worked out well for Vicky Nelson.

The middle child of Manfred and Edie Nelson, and the only girl among five siblings—Judy and Gary were seven and six years older, Dale and Bradley were three and six years younger, respectively—anytime the weather allowed it out on the front lawn of their Grove City house, Vicky could be found playing baseball, football, you name it. Hot Box was particularly popular when only some of the Nelson siblings were around. Picture a rundown in a baseball game, but when the runner is tagged out, the runner becomes a fielder, the fielder a runner, and the game continues.

Vicky's athleticism attracted the attention of one of Peps's scouts: her grandmother, who lived across the street from the Nelsons. "Her grandmother made the comment to her that hey, there's a little girl across the street, and she's kind of a little tomboy it looks like," Vicky said, laughing. "And then when Peps would come around for Easter or [other holidays], she would visit her grandmother quite a bit. And when she did, she'd organize a basketball game up at the basketball court."

Gary would usually play in those games, and Vicky soon joined in, a bit in awe of Peps, the older girl who'd made good, playing basketball in an au courant bouffant hairdo. But Vicky chose school over sports, and when Vicky headed for college, Peps didn't try to recruit her for the Gems—she respected her decision to go to school and didn't want to interfere with that.

But first at Willmar Community College, then at Moorhead State College—both in Minnesota—Vicky discovered that she liked basketball a lot more than she liked school. "I heard through the grapevine from her mother that she might think about quitting that last semester, and you know, it's just fate how these things happen," Peps said. "Because it just so happened that one of my players decided that they wanted to go into a different line of work. And so there was an opening, and I thought, *Well, why not give Vicky a chance?*"

So Peps walked across the street from her grandmother's house to the Nelsons' right after Christmas, and the deal was struck. Vicky Nelson joined the Gems.

Vicky thought of herself as a shy young woman, excited about basketball but nervous about showmanship, sensitive about a voice she thought of as "so nasally." Years later, she recalled herself at that moment and said that if there'd been a conventional basketball path, she would have taken it.

But a funny thing happened during her first month on the road with the Gems. Peps integrated her into every part of the show, including the halftime entertainment. And Vicky Nelson, it turned out, was a natural. "I was pretty shy at first," Vicky said. "And then I kind of came out of my shell. I would go to the locker room before the games and set up some of the skits with the guys that we were playing against. We had to have some that were set up. And then I would talk to the referees and all that, and I really gained confidence over probably the first month or so."

Peps turned over the halftime announcer's microphone to Vicky, then started letting Vicky do the halftime show itself. "She was the best microphone I ever had," Peps said. "Probably not the best player

I ever had—that would either be me or Judy Oelrich. But Vicky just fit the bill all the way around on doing everything."

A subtle but unmistakable change could be found in the way the Gems were written up as the 1970s proceeded. Gone was referring to the team as a novelty, as the only way for people around the country to watch women's basketball. The Association for Intercollegiate Athletics for Women (AIAW) began holding collegiate tournaments for women, and stars such as Lusia Harris at Delta State and Marianne Stanley at Immaculata drew notice—and big crowds.

The 1976 U.S. Olympic Basketball Team, led by Harris and Ann Meyers Drysdale and coached by Billie Moore, won the silver medal. The Women's Professional Basketball League (WBL) emerged in 1978 out of the success of USA Basketball, and not only were many of the Olympians part of that league, so were Minnesota legends who'd been barnstorming too, such as Lynnette Sjoquist. Eventually Sjoquist would lead the Minnesota Fillies to a quarterfinals victory over the New Orleans Pride at Williams Arena in Minneapolis—a venue that will come up again here.

Peps had turned down an offer from the WBL, as had her Arkansas Lassies teammate Linda Yearby—$25,000 up front, the other $25,000 during the season. Neuman liked her freedom, for one thing, and had real skepticism about whether a league could succeed financially at that time. Considering the Fillies had to walk off the court in Chicago to protest not getting their paychecks in their third and final season—a common occurrence, sadly, despite the WBL's incredible talent base and impact on women's basketball—that doesn't seem like a foolish decision.

Meanwhile, the *Verona–Cedar Grove Times* of New Jersey touted Peps's "hook shot from half court, a 35-foot swisher, twisting-driving lay-up, or free throws from her knees" ahead of a March 1978 appearance by the Gems in Verona.

As the Gems continued thrilling crowds in hundreds of cities and towns every year, even the occasional loss was sufficiently surprising to merit headlines. In the lead-up to a December 5, 1980, game in Lee, Massachusetts, the Lee High School alumni team's head coach, Ed Thomas, promised plenty of star power, and numerous male players who went on to play college basketball participated. Despite the seriousness with which they took things, and a big early lead, Lee barely held on to win 78–75. It was just the Gems' second loss in 163 games. "It happens now and then," Peps told the *Berkshire Eagle* after the game. "But the girls are walking out with their chins up." The two teams then celebrated the night's reward—a lot of money raised for a local scholarship fund—with a dinner at Greenock Country Club.

This traveling life was how Peps Neuman and Vicky Nelson spent their fall, winter, and spring every year. And crucially, Peps Sports, Incorporated, ran into the black every single year. So let's just take a moment and remember this for every bad-faith attack on women's basketball past, present, and future: a women-owned, women-created business featuring women's basketball players not only succeeded for a quarter of a century, but it made money every single year too.

But Peps wasn't content to stay home even in the summer, though the Neuman family farm became the base of operations for all the Gems, with teammates often coming and staying for weeks or months at a time. Neuman was still running the basketball concession on the Minnesota summer carnival circuit that she had started in 1971, and in time she would incorporate Vicky into that as well.

Whether it was nights together on the farm, laughter audible deep into Minnesota summer darkness—as Vicky said with a chuckle, "We were products, literally, of the Eden Valley Emil Neuman Farm System"—or the places they all got to visit, with sightseeing alongside basketball, it was a life that none of the Gems would have traded for anything. "I knew it was just a close-knit group. And you know, we did traveling together and sightseeing, and I knew that we'd always take time out to stop and smell the roses," Vicky said.

Peps and Vicky, along with the rest of the Gems, became huge Broadway theater buffs—an early trip to New York to see Carol Channing in *Hello, Dolly!* hooked them—and so Peps always made certain to schedule some games in close proximity to New York City every year. Peps's favorite production? *Same Time, Next Year.* Vicky was partial to Neil Simon's *Broadway Bound* trilogy, and remembered a teenage Matthew Broderick exiting the stage door after a performance they'd seen of *Brighton Beach Memoirs* and taking off down the street on his bicycle.

One could often see the Gems standing excitedly in the TKTS ticket line in Times Square, seeking their next theater fix, for matinees ahead of local game times. Like the night in 1983 they faced Lawrence Taylor and other players for the New York Giants in a benefit game at Westchester County College's fieldhouse, or the time in 1982 when Peps and the Gems overpowered an Iona College alumni team led by 6'10" Mike Ice 90–77. Peps had 38 points that night. She estimated her team traveled 50,000 miles that year. "I hadn't done much traveling,"

Vicky recalled. "So that was a big thrill. For the big trips, the over-nighters, it was usually Peps and I that did all the driving. And it got to be somewhat cumbersome. But come game time, it was worth it."

Halftime didn't stay static either. By the 1980s Vicky was a main-stay on the mic; Peps and Judy Oelrich took different tacks for the halftime entertainment. Sometimes the lights went off on purpose, because the Gems had a glow ball, and Peps's amazing ballhandling could be seen amid the darkness, wowing the crowd—"Raunchy" had given way, musically, to "Cabaret" by then. Or Judy would excite the fans with her juggling proclivity—two, then three basketballs, then three basketballs and an apple, then three basketballs while taking bites out of the apple.

Peps Neuman turned 40 in 1984. For other careers, that isn't particularly advanced. For basketball? It's practically unheard of to play much longer, if a player is still playing at that point at all. And while the Gems kept on making more money than they spent, and Peps averaged 36 points per game in 1986, according to the *Glens Falls Post-Star*, she started to think about what life might be like after the Gems. A big reason? Much of the ground she'd covered had led to the kind of progress that made her way of life more difficult. It would not be the last time this happened to a women's basketball trailblazer.

"When they started forming girls high school basketball teams, it got harder to book games," Vicky recalled. "Because, 'Oh, on Tuesday nights we have a girls' game.' . . . And the novelty was wearing off after a while because people could see their own high school teams play. If they wanted to watch girls play, they could do that whenever." And that wasn't the only change. Money and aging stepped into the conversation. "Expenses got to be a little bit more expensive—gas and hotels. And then we were getting a little bit older. The age thing kind of crept up on everybody," Vicky said. "But we were the last barnstorming team around. We held out longer than everybody else."

Peps saw how good the college game was getting—even the high school games she saw impressed her—and realized she had made it into her 40s with no major injuries. Sure, the pull of the road, the decade-plus she'd played with Vicky and Judy—it all held a special place in her heart. She'd proven that women's basketball could dazzle, playing by men's rules against men. If she was a victim of her own success—if the Gems were, at some level, obsolete by virtue of her own creativity and talent—it was a reality she took on with pride, not a burden to live with. "I never, ever, ever believed there would be a WNBA with girls making money or that they could live on their salary," Peps said. "Never thought that they could be in commercials and be on TV and all that. I never, ever dreamt that girls' basketball in itself would get this big. I'm just so proud."

And for Vicky, the recognition of what began with the Gems is clear to her every time she and Peps are sitting courtside for a women's basketball game and the halftime entertainment comes onto the floor, and it's third- and fourth-grade girls, playing the game at a high skill level, younger than Vicky was when she got introduced to basketball at all. "I definitely think we made an impact on women's sports and especially basketball," Vicky said. "Because you've got to start some-where. And we laid the foundation for the skill level now. . . . I'm almost kind of jealous, because they have all these neat little uniforms, the sneakers and the wristbands. But I mean, I'm actually not so much jealous. I just smile and say to myself, 'Yeah, well, we started something, anyway. Got things pointed in the right direction.'" Peps added, "If it wasn't for where it's grown to today, it wouldn't mean a thing that we were pioneers back then."

By the time Peps, Vicky, and the Gems prepared to take the floor at Eden Valley High School on April 28, 1988, Peps knew this would be her final game. That she was ending at home—after scoring more than 108,000 points and playing 3,100 games, with her jersey on display in the Basketball Hall of Fame and her legacy secure—all allowed her to feel as if the night were a celebration. She'd played her first game in Eden Valley as a Texas Cowgirl 26 years earlier. The Gems played their first game there as well, the first-ever game at the new gym in Eden Valley. It's named after Peps Neuman now, by the way, housing high school games for the same district once helmed by the superintendent who thought Peps was stupid for believing she could have a professional life in basketball.

Neuman and the Gems faced an area men's team. As so often happened, the Gems won, 96–82, with Peps scoring 28 points. Judy Oelrich added 25 in the win, which also featured Peps delivering the halftime entertainment with dribbling tricks done with a glow ball. "I guess I haven't found anything as exciting, because every night is a high," Peps told the *St. Cloud Times* that night. "If people get high on drugs like I get high on basketball, I can see why once they get addicted to drugs, they stay on them."

Peps's mother and father were in the crowd, cheering their youngest on, along with countless family members. Vicky remembered spotting her parents and oldest brother, Judy. So many friends joined in the celebration that continued long into the night, everyone heading to the Eden Valley Senior Center to celebrate Peps's long career.

Various discussions followed. Should Vicky or Judy Oelrich continue the team? Both ultimately decided that wasn't for them. Should
Peps sell the name? Ultimately Peps made the decision to end things
on her own terms. There'd be no continuing the Gems under other
circumstances, with someone at the helm who Peps worried wouldn't
approach it with the same level of professionalism.

But for 26 years, Peps Neuman created a place for herself, and so
many other young women, to play basketball and earn a living doing
it. That the Gems did not exist into perpetuity does not diminish
that incredible accomplishment. Still, the lack of permanence in the
women's game could be felt by everyone, Peps and Vicky included.
There was no pension for the Gems. Peps was still in her early 40s,
Vicky her early 30s. There was a life to live.

Peps took vacations to Hawaii and Texas. She continued to help
her mom on the Neuman family farm while living at her own place in
Clearwater, Minnesota. She and Vicky would rent a kiosk at the mall
up in Willmar, Minnesota, and sell framed artwork or photographs,
while continuing on the carnival circuit every summer.

And the farm itself continued to serve as a home for Gems past
and present, the team as Peps's second family, long after the final
whistle sounded. It was central to her identity, this sisterhood, and
just *how* central would become clearer in the years ahead.

But it still wasn't easy at first for Peps or Vicky to find a comfortable fit in the game they'd done as much as anyone to build once
their playing careers were complete. "The first couple of years when
I went to Eden Valley–Watkins girls' and boys' games, it was tough
for me to sit and watch them play because I thought I should be out
there," Peps remembered. "I could feel it."

Eventually Peps Neuman and Vicky Nelson found their home in the world of women's basketball again. But it took more building from the generations that followed. Even as the Gems played their final years, a young woman was finding herself 1,264 miles from Eden Valley, beginning a journey of her own that would change the landscape of women's basketball forever.

CHAPTER 3

CHERYL

———

W HILE IT TOOK JOINING THE TEXAS Cowgirls for Peps Neuman to leave the
state of Minnesota, Cheryl Reeve knew only the road throughout
her entire childhood. In fact, it wouldn't be until her 40s that she'd
find the level of sustainable success as a head coach in the game that
turned Minnesota into not only a destination for women's basketball
but an exemplar for how the most successful teams would operate.

Cheryl was born to Larry and Rae Reeve on September 20, 1966,
in Omaha, Nebraska. She had two brothers: Larry Jr., 13 months
older than her, and Tom, 2 years younger than her. The Reeve family lived the transitory life made necessary by Larry's tenure in the
air force. Cheryl was born just steps from Offutt Air Force Base, and
the Reeve family stayed until Cheryl was nine, when they picked up
and moved to Georgia. Three years later, new orders came through:
Alaska. Cheryl remembered that her dad acquired a camper, and the
Reeve family was set to take on the new adventure when the orders
changed: Japan was to be the new destination.

The air force was a calling for Larry. But he made a decision to keep his kids in the United States and retired at the level of sergeant after two decades in the service. It was a decision that would change the direction of Cheryl's life, and women's basketball, as a result.

It is certainly possible that nothing would have prevented Cheryl from pursuing basketball as her lifelong calling, as surely as the air force served that purpose for Larry. She grew up at a time when Title IX—signed the summer of the year she turned six—had transformed the national conversation around women's sports.

In October 1975, the year Cheryl moved to Georgia, journalist Patricia Anstett wrote about the state of the game: "More high school and college women are dedicated to the game and gaining fans, and eight- and nine-year-olds are clamoring to be the next Jacky Chazalon, France's female basketball superstar whose left and right hook shots have made sports news around the world."

"This thing is absolutely mushrooming; it's absolutely amazing what has happened to women's basketball in the last five years," Patricia Kennedy, who pioneered a girls' basketball camp along with Immaculata College head coach Cathy Rush, told Anstett. The number of girls playing basketball in this country doubled, to 203,000, from 1971 to 1973. (You guessed it: Title IX was signed on June 23, 1972.) Patricia would go on to, among other things, start the Wade Trophy, a national player of the year award for the best in women's college basketball each season since 1977.

But as always with women's basketball, any progress comes with both a backlash from the outside and the understanding within the game that it is necessary to simultaneously be proud of the distance traveled and yet dissatisfied and motivated by how far there is still to go.

The women's game was not unique at this point to the Gems; it also applied to the All-American Red Heads and other early pioneers. But it was far from universal, and it is taken as a given in Anstett's story that the treatment of girls' and women's teams was far worse than that of those teams on the opposite side of the sexual divide when examined through the lens of the budget, attention, and intentionality boys' and men's basketball received as a birthright.

Chazalon, the future International Basketball Federation (FIBA) Hall of Famer, drew just nine mentions total in 1975 newspapers archived at Newspapers.com. Cheryl had not even heard of her; few people had. The growth of the women's game was happening simultaneously all over the world but was siloed, and it was occurring quickly in some places—where agents of change could collaborate with forward-thinking people in places of power—but infuriatingly slowly elsewhere.

So when Larry Sr. decided to retire from the air force, he and his wife, Rae, decided to return to their south New Jersey roots and moved the family to Washington Township. And Cheryl, 15 years old at this point, found herself in the middle of a high school basketball dynasty in the making.

The Philadelphia area itself had become an incubator for women's basketball. Cathy Rush (pride of Egg Harbor, New Jersey), paced by her lightning-quick point guard Marianne Stanley and intimidating center Theresa Grentz, won three straight national titles from 1972 to 1974 with Immaculata before falling to Lusia Harris and Delta State in the 1975 national final. Both Grentz and Stanley went on to long, celebrated careers as coaches themselves, each earning entry into the Women's Basketball Hall of Fame.

To put the coaching dominance of this trio in perspective: The AIAW awarded 11 national championships in women's college basketball. Rush (three with Immaculata), Stanley (two with Old Dominion), and Grentz (one with Rutgers) captured more than half of them. And the Philadelphia/South Jersey area has produced more coaching talent than it is possible to list here. South Carolina court architect Dawn Staley hails from North Philly. Notre Dame coaching legend Muffet McGraw, from Pottsville, Pennsylvania, played for Stanley at St. Joseph's in Philly. Connecticut's Geno Auriemma, from nearby Norristown, Pennsylvania, got his first coaching gig as an assistant at St. Joseph's, and his top assistant since 1988 (and alter ego, really) is Chris Dailey, a New Jersey product who played for Grentz on the Rutgers title team in 1982. She's in the Women's Basketball Hall of Fame too.

From 2013 to 2023, the NCAA awarded 10 national championships in women's basketball. Staley, McGraw, and Auriemma combined to win seven of them, and South Carolina finished atop the 2019–20 Associated Press rankings, though no tournament was held due to COVID–19.

So to call the area a haven for women's basketball, then and now, is an understatement. And the house the Reeves moved into by the 1981–82 season, Cheryl's sophomore year in high school, was less than a half hour's drive to that mecca of Philadelphia basketball, the Palestra. So Reeve, who grew up playing first baseball, then softball, field hockey, a little soccer, and basketball, did not have to introduce the game to her Washington Township High School as Peps had to hers.

Not with Chuck Earling, the school's longtime athletic director and so-called Mr. Washington Township, overseeing athletics and always making sure the girls' teams got what they needed. He eventually married Margaret Hodge, a multisport athlete at Washington Township. Even so, Cheryl remembered that the boys always got access to the main gym, with more baskets to work on skills, while the girls ended up in the auxiliary gym. Always that balance between measuring progress and seeing that gap in inequality persist.

As for Cheryl's own desire? No one needed to do a thing, even if her habit of keeping a comb in her sock and combing out her unruly blonde hair during practices sometimes infuriated her coach. "She was always self-motivated," Rae Reeve told Kent Youngblood of the *Minneapolis Star Tribune* back in 2013. "Always driven to be the best, no matter what." That manifested itself in one-on-one basketball games on the Reeves' hoop bolted onto the house in their driveway, and home run derby competitions with Tom that, he recalled years later, Cheryl would declare done once she was ahead. "She being older, she'd say, 'Sorry, it's time to eat,'" Tom remembered.

That desire to be the best was the first thing her new teammates at Washington Township High School noticed about her. "Gritty, scrawny," Kim Franchi, who was two years ahead of Reeve at Washington Township High School, recalled. "Really terrible attitude. Hated to lose. She would fly off the handle and walk out of the gym any second if you let her."

But the coach of Cheryl's Washington Township team, Dawn Shilling, didn't let her out of the gym, nor did Shilling's teams lose very much. Her installation at coach wasn't an accident, as another teammate of Franchi's and Reeve's, Karen Healey (now Karen Healey Lange), remembered. "[Some players' dads] went to Mr. Earling before our ninth grade year and said, 'Look, no offense to the current coach. She's a nice lady. But you have a lot of talent coming up,'" Healey Lange recalled. "'And we're hoping that—' There were no threats. It wasn't confrontational to Mr. Earling when they said it; he was such a nice guy. But you know, you have to give credit to the dads who said, 'You really need to explore putting in a different type of coach.'"

Earling hired Shilling from just up the road at Glassboro State in 1979. She brought a modern sensibility to the game, deploying both a full-court press and a 1–3–1 half-court trap defense as the situations allowed, and a practice routine that the players universally loathed—at least, until they saw what it did for them in games. "We try to steal the ball up top," Washington Township center Kelly DeLong told the *Courier-Post* in January 1982. "This year we really have the speed to run. She runs us a lot in practice. We hate it, but it pays off. We're one of the best-conditioned teams in the conference."

It made for some lopsided scores—the Washington Township Minutemen beat Williamstown High School 100–6 that year—but this was a powerhouse team no matter how the game unfolded. DeLong, the center, went on to play at Missouri. Healey Lange, perhaps the best player in school history, graduated and starred at Temple. Ross played softball and field hockey, earning All-State honors in both sports while scoring more than 1,000 points in basketball. She went on to play softball and field hockey at North Carolina. And Franchi, the tough-as-nails senior on that 1982 team, eventually played basketball and softball at Glassboro State. She wouldn't let her high school team lose, even on the rare occasions opponents could slow the Minutemen down, such as when she hit a 23-footer in the final second to beat Edgewood 50–48, improving Washington Township's record to 15–1. (In 2020 NJ.com made a "Mount Rushmore" for Washington Township athletics. Ross and Healey Lange were two of the four selected.)

Washington Township easily won its conference, finishing 23–3, and only losing to the top-ranked team in the state, Atlantic City, led by Atlantic City High School's all-time leading scorer, Valeria Jones. Shilling's pick to guard her was Cheryl, and she held her to four points in the first half, before a second-half bout with foul trouble forced her to back off. The Minutemen finished one defeat short of a chance to play for the sectional title, and lost Franchi and DeLong to graduation. (A little more than a month later, Reeve, playing for Shilling in softball, set the school record for stolen bases.)

The following basketball season, they were even better. Healey Lange scored 22 and Washington Township avenged the loss from the year before 53–33. The two-time defending state champions had been vanquished.

The toughness of this team is perhaps best exemplified by a night Cheryl and Kim Franchi were driving home from Cherry Hill Summer League basketball. It had been a hard-fought game between the players still in school, such as Reeve, Franchi, and Healey Lange, and some older vets in the area, including Deirdre Kane (Camden Catholic, South Jersey's 1976 College Player of the Year, who played at Dayton) and Valerie Still (Cherry Hill East, Kentucky's all-time leading scorer, who eventually played in the WNBA). Cheryl got popped in the face during the game, and said casually on the car ride home, "Hey, Franchi, my nose kind of hurts." So the two of them went to the ER, where they saw the other people coming in—pregnant ladies, people with wounds—and decided they didn't need to stick around. Of course, as soon as Cheryl walked in the door to her house, her parents noticed her badly broken nose and took her right back to the hospital. But she was prepared to keep going as if nothing had happened.

Washington Township won the sectional title in 1984, and in signature fashion—in better shape than their opponents, Southern High School, the Minutemen climbed back from a six-point deficit with 4:33 to go, forced overtime on a Healey Lange 10-footer, and won 51–46 in the extra period. The defense and rebounding meant that Washington Township took 60 field-goal attempts to Southern's 31.

There was no rest, though. The group transitioned seamlessly from basketball to softball, just as they had field hockey to basketball when fall season turned to winter. "We grew up in an era where you just always played a sport," Healey Lange said. "That was just my family's life."

This was the social life of the group as well. There'd be occasional trips to the movies, or McDonald's, or Friendly's—"Friendly's was big for us," Cheryl recalled—but ask Cheryl or Kim or Karen what they remember, and it is playing sports, particularly basketball, with a loyalty that would continue decades into the future, and a distaste for opponents that lives on to this day. Healey Lange said she can't quite get her mind around it when she sees opponents hugging before games. "We should be kicking their ass! You can hug them later, after you kick their ass. But the kids nowadays are so nice," Healey Lange lamented. And the added edge was necessary. "She was my bodyguard," Healey Lange said of Franchi, the 5'7" forward with no vertical leap who led Washington Township in rebounding her senior season on sheer will. "Because people wanted to literally kill me."

It is a mentality that Cheryl Reeve took into her future endeavors. And that path would be basketball, even though by her own accounting, she was a better softball player. She'd received more letters from coaches in softball too. And she believes the reason Division I coaches saw her play basketball primarily was due to her surrounding teammates, such as the Temple-bound Healey Lange. But Dawn sat Cheryl down during her senior year in 1984 and told her that there'd be significantly more scholarship money to be found in basketball than softball.

As she looks back years later, Cheryl isn't so much filled with disappointment with the path chosen—"The basketball thing worked out okay for me," she said, laughing—as she is that the limits of her path were dictated in a way she didn't even question at the time. "Because of what we talk about now, what I've been part of and advocate for . . . something that bothers me the most is that it was just reality for us. So I didn't think twice to question it. It was just a coach telling me, 'This is the way it is. And we are accepting it.' That's the way it is. . . . And maybe [that's] the mindset, like it is many times with women: 'Well, at least we're progressing.' Instead of saying, 'This isn't right,' it was more of, 'Twelve years ago, we didn't have this.'"

So it was off to La Salle University for Cheryl, right in the heart of Philadelphia, to play for the Explorers. She'd been recruited by Kevin Gallagher. "Kevin was the only coach who recruited me," Reeve recalled a few years later to the *Philadelphia Inquirer*. "It was either La Salle or go to work." But the fiery Philadelphia boys' high school coach Bill "Speedy" Morris, took over the La Salle women's program in time for Cheryl's freshman year.

Cheryl's consciousness-raising continued at La Salle. The differences inherent in the men's and women's basketball program did not escape her notice, for instance. "We played in the MAAC, the Metro Atlantic Athletic Conference, at that time," Reeve said. "And so a lot of what the men did—when we would go play Fordham, we'd play on a Saturday, say at two PM, so we would get up, get on a bus at eight AM, and we would drive the bus up to the Bronx. Get off the bus, go warm up for the game, play the game, get on the bus, and come home. And the guys went up the night before. That was always a big thing—that we said the guys got the chance to go up, stay overnight, get a good night's sleep, and then wake up the next day and go play their game. So that was a fundamental difference."

Despite the gaps in treatment, though, Reeve said the glorious renaissance for basketball at La Salle, enjoying the time of Tim Legler and Lionel "L-Train" Simmons on the men's side, carried over into the women's program. La Salle is not a place with massive facilities or deep-pocketed alums, but the collective efforts to fundraise made a difference, and Cheryl's era of Explorers basketball was a successful one.

The hierarchy was never clearer, though, than in March 1986, when Reeve's La Salle team fell to Harry Perretta's Villanova Wildcats in the first round of the NCAA tournament. The *Philadelphia Daily News* had a story about the game, of course—it was the first win in the NCAA tournament by any Big East women's basketball team, but not the last, with first-year Connecticut coach Geno Auriemma beginning his tenure with the Huskies in 1985–86 at 12–15.

But above the *Daily News* story was Speedy Morris expressing interest—at the postgame of the NCAA tournament game with the La Salle women—in moving to the just-vacated La Salle men's job. "My philosophy is, 'I'm here and they know what I can do,'" Morris said that day. "If the people on the school's athletic committee approach me, sure I'd be interested."

Players, Reeve included, were publicly supportive of a coach they loved at the time. In retrospect, though, the full picture is much clearer to her. "I do remember being very, very disappointed when Speedy made the move over to the men's program," Reeve told KYW News-radio in 2021. "Then I thought, *Gosh, how naive were we at that age that—of course that was a setup for him to get the men's job.* I know a lot more now than what we knew then. But I look back and I go, 'That whole thing was planned.' I enjoyed the time that we had with Speedy, and I'm very thankful for it." But she added, "Then there's times I'm a little irritated that the women's program was used in that way. Again, knowing a lot more now."

Her new coach, John Miller, was a different presence on the bench, a calm antidote to Morris and his manic exhortations. Back in Cheryl's freshman year, Morris actually made her cry—something almost inconceivable to those who know the tough-exteriored Lynx coach today. Reeve said:

> My first season, as a freshman, I actually had the opportunity to start because the senior Gina Tobin was injured. And I probably wasn't ready. Speedy was, you know, obviously really demanding. And [we were] down at Delaware. My first game [was] La Salle versus Delaware, and Delaware was in this zone, a 2–3 zone, and they weren't guarding me at the top and they kind of spread out on the wings, and I just repeatedly was taking turns on which side [to throw to] and turning the ball over, [and I] ended up with nine turnovers.

Speedy finally had enough and sat me down and—I've actually recently told our players this story—I began to cry. And Speedy turned and looked at me, and he said, "*You're* crying? *You're* crying? *I* should be crying!"

It was the same kind of tough love Cheryl grew up experiencing from her father. She had vivid memories of walking back to the car after softball games, her father (usually her head coach) yelling at her about a play not made, her mother chiming in to tell her she didn't have to keep playing if she preferred to stop. She never did, though.

Under Miller, she would thrive, scoring 12 points, including a game-winning three-point play, in a 50–49 victory over St. Joseph's in a Big 5 contest on December 23, 1987, that her coach described afterward as "a war." She won Big 5 Player of the Week honors for her effort.

By the early part of 1988, Reeve's senior season at La Salle, the low-scoring guard at Washington Township had been the Explorers' engine for her entire career. That season she scored 19 in a game at Fordham, leading all scorers. At Delaware, there was no crying, just leading all scorers again with 18, and adding 8 rebounds.

A month later, standing at center court of La Salle's Hayman Hall, she received a bouquet of flowers and a plaque commemorating her 100th career start, the first Explorer ever to reach that mark. She finished her career with 110, which is tied for third-most in program history, while her 420 assists rank sixth all-time in La Salle history. Her former coach, Dawn Shilling, was on hand to see it and said that day: "She was never in the limelight, but if you came to our games, you would not forget Cheryl."

In early March Cheryl scored 29 in Jersey City to beat St. Peter's and improve La Salle's record to 23–3. The Explorers were now ranked 20th in the country. Reeve was leading the nation in free throw shooting, at 92 percent. She hit two of them to seal that road win. It earned her Big 5 Player of the Week honors again too.

La Salle made the NCAA tournament that March, along with fellow Big 5 teams Villanova and St. Joe's. Lisa Angelotti won Big East Player of the Year. Reeve was All-MAAC first-team. Her reward? Having to try and slow down Suzie McConnell Serio of Penn State, a 5'4" wunderkind of a point guard, who entered the tournament averaging 20.3 points per game. For the first 27 minutes or so it worked, with Reeve blanketing McConnell and getting the Explorers out to an 11-point lead.

But Reeve got crushed on a back screen around the 13-minute mark, and was likely concussed. She continued playing—it was 1988, after all—but McConnell went *off*, scoring 17 of the next 26 points for Penn State. Ultimately the overflow crowd at Hayman Hall saw La Salle fall to Penn State 86–85. (A fun historical footnote: The only two Minnesota Lynx coaches in franchise history to win WNBA Coach of the Year? Suzie McConnell Serio and Cheryl Reeve.)

That very same day as the 86–85 loss to Penn State, Angelotti's collegiate career ended as well, with Villanova's loss to Wake Forest. And just like that, the promise of Title IX crashed into the reality of the still-undeveloped women's basketball infrastructure faced by young women who would otherwise be lifers in the sport.

Let's just take a moment and consider what opportunities would have been available to Cheryl Reeve and Lisa Angelotti in 2023. Reeve, a national leader in free throw shooting and floor general for an NCAA tournament team, a coach on the floor and tenacious defender who could score, even if scoring was not her primary skill set, sounds a lot like the seventh pick in the 2023 WNBA Draft, Grace Berger, from Indiana University (selected by the Indiana Fever). Berger grew up going to Fever games, and as of summer 2023, she was essentially playing for her hometown team.

The Angelotti comp in the 2023 draft is even easier: Maddy Siegrist. Like Angelotti, Siegrist won Big East Player of the Year honors as a scoring forward at Villanova. For that storied career and potential, there was never a doubt that she'd have a WNBA future, and the Dallas Wings selected her with the third overall pick in the 2023 WNBA Draft, while Siegrist was quickly added to the Puma family of athletes, along with endorsement deals from places such as SoFi bank and Urban Outfitters.

Contrast that with the *actual* immediate futures of Reeve and Angelotti back in 1988. In April the two were honored at the Albert J. Carino Basketball Club of South Jersey in Cherry Hill. That night at the Hyatt, both considered their basketball futures. Angelotti was resigned to it all ending. "I can't believe it's all over," she told the *Courier-Post* that night. "I've been playing since I was five. To have it just stop all of a sudden . . . it's hard. But every athlete's career has to end, and this is mine. Now I can start being a nurse."

It's hard not to hear this and contrast it with Siegrist's path. Siegrist got a master's in education at Villanova. She'd have been a teacher. But she loved the game like Angelotti did, and instead, 400 of her closest family and friends packed multiple sections of Barclays Center a few weeks after she was drafted to cheer her on in her pro career, just a short train ride from where Siegrist grew up in Poughkeepsie.

As for Reeve? The outlook was even cloudier. She'd been a computer science major—the deal with her parents was that they'd pay for school and her dad would pick her major—and she wanted no part of going to play overseas. Her backcourt mate Kelly Greenberg went to Australia, but Reeve couldn't conceive of it. She wanted something pretty basic: At age 22, with the gift of basketball knowledge accumulated over a lifetime, she wanted to pursue that profession, either playing or coaching here in the United States. By the time she'd coached at the Cathy Rush Basketball Camp during the summer of her junior and senior years at La Salle, coaching was the only life she knew would make her happy.

And yet it took almost two decades before that looked and felt less like an unrealistic dream and more like a reasonable path, even for the most successful coach of her generation. Coming out of school, she had another in a series of conversations with her parents, her dad urging her to give up on the idea of coaching and find something more stable. They reached detente thanks to her coach at La Salle, John Miller, who offered her a graduate assistant position while Reeve returned to school to get a master's degree.

"Thankfully I chose that path to go get a master's and I got an MBA with a specialization in human resource management, because I thought that most would resemble coaching. Somehow that was my logic at that time," Reeve recalled with a chuckle. "It has absolutely nothing to do with coaching, but at the time, I reasoned that's why I was going to go get an MBA. Because I thought, *I don't know what the hell I want to do. Go get it, go get an MBA or master's in something.* But that's what I did. It was a great decision. Like my mom said, I have this master's and that high level of education." She added, "It probably all served me well, but more than anything, it got me down this path of being a coach. All the way up until 2008, when my dad passed, he asked me every year when I was going to get a real job."

The same reality followed Karen Healey the following April, after she led her Temple Owls into the second round of the NCAA tournament. In an April 1989 event at that same Cherry Hill Hyatt mentioned earlier, she pondered a life without basketball, even though she too had the passion and the mind for it. As Bob Brookover wrote in the *Courier-Post* about her on March 30, 1989: "She'd like to stay in the game in some capacity, but she's not sure how."

This was, indeed, the reality baked into the limitations of Title IX in both implementation and infrastructure built around it as the 1980s gave way to the 1990s. For Peps Neuman and Vicky Nelson, who found a loophole to build playing careers, there was no clear way to continue engaging with the sport as a coach or any other role when they'd finished playing. For Reeve, Healey, Angelotti, and Franchi, the last of whom picked up some coaching gigs assisting at Triton High School and had a brief stint coaching softball at Glassboro State, even that path was beyond their easy grasp. Franchi won New Jersey Athletic Conference Coach of the Year in her second season as softball coach, Glassboro State having changed its name to Rowan University. She was doing it part-time, and continued part-time the following year as she won Division III Middle Atlantic Coach of the Year, the Rowan University Profs a national power. Even Angelotti, who became the head coach at Gloucester Catholic High School—and at the time of this writing is coaching Healey Lange's daughter Katherine—never stopped her work as a full-time nurse as she did so. Healey Lange got a degree in criminal justice, took the LSATs, and ended up working for U.S. Healthcare.

Two decades into Title IX, the simple ask—to make a career of the craft they'd spent their entire childhoods honing—was a bridge too far. "I was involved in coaching," Franchi said. "The pay wasn't really there. . . . I just kind of thought that it really wasn't worth it anymore because of the [lack of] opportunities for women."

Franchi's only year full-time, her salary was $35,145. She was suspended that season, however, over an incident in which she caught her players out of their hotel rooms on the road and was accused of shoving them amid trying to get them back into their rooms. Despite tearful pleas from former players and Franchi alike, Rowan University fired Franchi. A men's coach anywhere close to as successful as Franchi probably would have weathered the incident, and certainly would have had other schools lining up to hire him.

"We always talk about this as female athletes," Healey Lange said of her friend. "There's been a lot of male coaches at the professional level, at the college level, who have had a bad departure, and they end up somewhere else within a year. And you just don't see the same frequency of those occurrences for females."

Even Reeve's path was bumpy, remarkable in retrospect considering the success she's gone on to have. After two years as a graduate assistant with John Miller at La Salle, MBA in tow (which she intended to do absolutely nothing with), Reeve got hired by another Philly guy, Joe McKeown, as an assistant at George Washington University. McKeown heard about Reeve from Morris and Miller.

The pipeline in Philadelphia—an infrastructure built ad hoc in many ways—launched Reeve.

Reeve said:

> I was so green, entering as a full-time assistant coach down at George Washington. But we spent five years together, Joe McKeown and I did. Joe transformed that program and gave me opportunities probably about my third year into being an assistant. I started getting opportunities because the program was so successful. We were ranked nationally, and I got some opportunities from what I would consider more BCS, bigger schools. [I] had maybe an opportunity to go to Arkansas and be in the SEC as assistant coach, so I had to make a decision. Was that my next step? Or did I want to be a head coach from my experience with GW?
>
> And Joe was really, really good at communicating with me about, "Hey, be careful what you wish for." Sometimes being a top assistant at a really good program like a George Washington—where we were recruiting well, we were having success—sometimes that's better than going to be head coach at a smaller program and having a hard time finding success. You don't have the resources, etc. So I was really mindful of that.
>
> It wasn't until after the fifth season—and at that point, we were ranked sixth in the country—that I really started to think I should strike while the iron was hot. An opportunity came for me to go coach at Indiana State. You know, when I look back on that, I thought that I was really in tune to the messaging from Joe McKeown. I think, having more worldly experience now, I probably would not have made that move. But it's something that I did. I was 28 years old.

Becoming a head coach at 28 was pretty young, I'd say. And no, I don't think I was ready.

Ready is a two-way term here. At 28 Cheryl Reeve became a Division I head coach of the Indiana State Sycamores, plugged into a Missouri Valley Conference filled with coaching talent. The Big Four coaches at that time? Cheryl Burnett at Southwest Missouri State (later head coach at Michigan); Jill Hutchison, the 28-year head coach at Illinois State; Cindy Scott, who coached at Southern Illinois University for 21 years and reached a Sweet 16 in 1987 amid eight 20-win seasons; and Lisa Bluder, who coached at Drake for 10 years, and since 2000 has been at Iowa, with a trip to the national title game in 2023, helping to earn her an extension in the summer of 2023 that runs through 2029. Together those four have won 2,021 games and counting entering the 2023–24 season, with Bluder almost assured to reach 1,000 wins alone by the time her current contract is complete.

"So those four kicked my ass," Reeve remembered. "They showed me, 'Hey, young gun.' And I was an idiot. I was, again, competitive and cocky and probably could have handled myself better during that time. But I learned a ton. But I also didn't want to back down. I wanted to let them know that I was there to do what they were doing."

Indiana State finished 7–19 in Reeve's first year. As she told the *Philadelphia Daily News* back in 1996, "It was a tough transition. I had always been in winning situations. When you're sitting at the assistant's desk, you dream about 20-win seasons. It was hard keeping the staff and the players together. I kidded Joe, 'You didn't prepare me for this.' When the horn sounded after the final game, it was a sigh of relief. We all felt, 'Now we'll build from here.'"

Years later, she put it more succinctly: "It was hell."

But for Cheryl Reeve, the itinerant child turned Jersey product, coming to the Midwest offered other culture shocks as well. Her East Coast intensity, she said, rubbed some people the wrong way in Indiana—a surprise to her, assuming this would simply be the women's version of Bob Knight and Larry Bird's approach to basketball.

And her very identity itself produced conflict. She was a lesbian, and even years after she'd found peace with it herself, and come out to her family and friends, being a lesbian coaching women's basketball in the 1990s was still fraught. "Your personal life is something that [was] very private [at that time] because, you know, it's like they say when you're getting arrested: 'Anything you say or do can be used against you,'" Reeve said. "Well, in recruiting, anything you are, or they think you might be, can be used against you."

Cheryl remembered knowing she was a lesbian by the time she entered high school:

> You know how you feel. But you don't want people to not like you, or you don't want people to shun you, [especially] your family. And so that's a lot. And so then you kind of go, "Okay. Well, I want my parents to be proud of me." So I'll go date this guy. Or whatever. Go to the movies. . . . Many people have this story where they just try, because who picks a life of being discriminated against at every turn? Because you're taught that what you're doing isn't right.
>
> And especially for someone like [me] . . . I wanted to be good at everything. I wanted to please. You want your

parents to be proud of you. We worked really hard to be great students. And we worked hard in sports. And they were proud of us. That was one place where you didn't want to let people down. And you certainly didn't want to embarrass them. You know? At family functions, you didn't want to be the outcast. You're just taught—you're just taught to hide it. And you're taught that it's not okay.

That is not to say her family said it wasn't okay or shunned her. There's no story in the Cheryl Reeve history of a big, dramatic reveal or getting thrown out of her house. Her father came to her when she was 15 or 16, "tried to do the right thing and asked [her]," and she was too scared to answer. So what happened next was everyone simply accepted the way things were. "I just lived," she said. "And I would bring my significant other around. And it was like, everybody knew. . . . My youngest brother and I, we would probably spend more time [together], and my older brother was very supportive. But I never had this conversation of, 'Hey, Mom and Dad.' I just never did it. I just lived. I feel like that's what I've always done. I've just kind of lived."

And so Reeve tried to replicate that "just living" in Indiana. There was no Jersey Shore in Indiana, the breeze of Ocean City in her hair on summer nights at her aunt's house, so she got herself a Wave-Runner, found some lakes, would decompress from the stress from coaching very occasionally with a girlfriend and a small group of friends. There were no secrets there. But there were no mentions on her Indiana State bio, no one around to upset the delicate balancing act at the press conference.

"There was no being out," Reeve said. "You couldn't live the way that heterosexual couples could live. You couldn't share very much because you knew that if something got out, then there would be people that would pounce on that." That fight was still to come.

Despite all these headwinds at Indiana State, this is still Cheryl Reeve we're talking about, so the winning came soon after—14–13 in 1996–97, 17–11 in 1997–98, 18–11 and a trip to the Women's National Invitation Tournament (WNIT) in 1998–99. They beat Illinois State, Southern Illinois and, at last, Drake that season. The intensity? That came along for the ride as well.

"We had some good battles when I was at Drake and Cheryl was at Indiana State," Bluder recalled in an email. "I remember one time I really made Cheryl mad at me. We lost at Indiana State (which didn't happen often), and Cheryl was pretty happy about the win. I was five months pregnant and pretty hormonal. I went off on the team . . . was pretty crazy, I believe. . . . I took forever in the locker room, and Cheryl was so mad that I didn't go to the presser afterward when she had 'finally' gotten us. She was cussing up a storm, according to my sports information director."

It is not to say that there weren't joyful moments along the way. Reaching the WNIT felt like tangible progress to Reeve—"Whether it's the Big Dance or the Little Dance, we're still dancing," she told the *Indianapolis Star* in March 1999. But the collective battle was taking a toll on Reeve. After a down year in 1999–2000, Reeve's Sycamores were off to a 1–3 start in 2000–01 when Reeve surprised everybody by deciding it was time to step down.

"Shocked would be a better description," then–Indiana State athletic director Andrea Myers told the *Indianapolis Star* that December. "We had had no discussions like, 'You have got to get it together.' We had some discussions over general stuff, but often in athletics there is no more pressure than coaches put on themselves."

But Myers identified the very thing that led Reeve to quit, and ultimately has driven much of her success before and since. "And people who are as competitive as Cheryl Reeve is put a lot of pressure on themselves. I think she didn't believe she was connecting with the team anymore, and she couldn't go through a whole season like that," Myers told the *Indianapolis Star* in the same interview.

Reeve was under no illusions that it would be easy to find another job, either. At 34, quitting in-season at a mid-major wasn't the ticket to long-term job security, particularly for a woman in coaching. "Obviously now is not the time to be looking for a job," she said at a farewell news conference. "But I love coaching and I feel like I have a chance to be successful in this profession. Hopefully it will work out."

Reeve had already seen a place that might offer the combination of intensity and professionalism she was seeking. Following her second year at Indiana State, a new professional women's basketball league, the WNBA, tipped off—first in eight U.S. cities but by 2000 in Indiana too. Reeve became a season-ticket holder to watch Anne Donovan's Indiana Fever expansion team.

Donovan couldn't do it alone, though. And her partner in building the paradigm for what sustainable professional women's basketball looked like, along with the point guard she'd need to achieve the kind of success on the court she'd always sought, were charting parallel courses in school, even as Reeve continued the conversations back home in New Jersey with her father about just how she planned to make a living coaching women's basketball. Meanwhile, Vicky Nelson faced a tragedy that changed her life, and that of Peps Neuman, forever.

CHAPTER 4

THE TEAM HOUSE

———

I**N ORDER TO UNDERSTAND** what happened next in the lives of Peps Neuman and Vicky Nelson, it is necessary to isolate two truths that have animated Peps Neuman's entire life. One is that if something needs doing, she does it. She doesn't wait, ask for permission, or consider how big the task ahead of her might be. It needs to be done, she sees a way, she does it. There was no other pathway to playing professional basketball for 26 years. So Peps Neuman created one. And when she saw ways to do it better, she did it herself.

The other thing is the concept of family for Peps. In the same way that Peps has always approached life when absolutely certain of her path—as a task to be conquered—she also shies away from what she doesn't believe is God's path for her. And from an early age, despite loving her nieces and nephews, Peps did not believe she was temperamentally suited to having children.

In an extended letter Peps wrote to me on her thoughts about family, she explained:

> Around the age of 19 or 20, I realized that God put me on this earth to entertain and to play basketball. I think even if I was a secretary or had a regular stay-at-home job, I would not have had a family. A lot of people are happy without children. At the time, I didn't think I had the patience and knowledge to raise a child to have the correct benefits of life.
>
> Nothing is more precious than a child on earth. I've heard [of] a lot of families having children, and have a disagreement, and never talk to them again or the children move far, far away. I just couldn't take that.

Nor did her teammates ever stop being her teammates. The family farm was no longer a training camp for the Gems, but it served as a place where longtime Gems would come and stay for days, even weeks. Emil passed away in 1993. Anna, now older and in need of a place to live that could accommodate a person who needed a walker, moved in with Peps, and Peps took on much of her caregiving. But the two of them were hardly ever alone. "We call it the Team House," Vicky said of Peps's house. "And anybody who ever wanted to stay, she was open to that."

This was just a natural extension of how Neuman viewed family. As Peps put it: "My basketball teammates were my family, and my relatives liked them too. I still had my mom and dad and my brothers and their families as my loving family. And I cannot forget my furry cats that gave me and give me love, as I spend a lot of time with them."

Peps and Vicky collaborated in business too—a framing kiosk in the mall during the fall, winter, and spring, and summers on the Minnesota fair circuit, operating a basketball shooting contest. People still challenged Peps or Vicky at the fairs, and the games generally went the way contests did against the Gems: many more made baskets for Peps or Vicky.

It was that concession—a high basket and wood frame that needed to be hauled with a trailer and a tilt bed pulled by a van and manually rebuilt at each new stop—that Vicky was driving over to a carnival in Wisconsin on the night of May 24, 2000. Peps was attending a funeral and planned to meet her the next day. Vicky was driving on Route 694 and noticed the tilt bed was starting to come up, indicating that the pin keeping the concession in place was coming loose. "Oh my god, I'm going to have lumber all over the freeway," Vicky recalled thinking.

She pulled over, but the spot she chose had a dip to it, and the already loosened pin gave way. The concession, and the van with Vicky in it, flipped over. Her initial fears were that the van would catch fire with her trapped in it. But she couldn't escape for another reason: she had no feeling in her legs. "I knew I was going to be paralyzed," she said. Within two to three minutes, she estimates, others had come along and called 911, and the paramedics were able to extricate her using the Jaws of Life. As they took her to Regions Hospital in St. Paul, they asked Vicky whom to call. The answer, of course, was Peps and Vivian, Vicky's mother. The two of them raced down to the hospital.

"We had no idea what we were getting into," Peps said. "We found out how serious it was, that it was a spinal cord injury. I thought, *That's not so bad*; I thought a broken neck was worse than a spinal cord injury. But I was wrong, I was so naive. I didn't know anything about it."

Vicky spent around six weeks in the hospital, but her spinal cord had been badly damaged, with many surgeries and residual pain to come in the years ahead. She'd never walk unaided again. So by the end of June 2000, when the hospital released her, the question arose of just where she'd go. Vivian was happy to take her in, of course, but wasn't really set up to care for someone with Vicky's needs. And at Vivian's age, that wasn't a long-term solution. There was, however, the Team House. "Well, if it wasn't for [Peps], I'm sure I would have been institutionalized," Vicky said. "Because who would give up all their time to take care of somebody that was in a wheelchair or a walker?"

But the way Peps saw it, there wasn't anything else to do but this. In her view, Vicky was family, and this was the only way forward. "My mom had a walker, and she was already living at my house," Peps said. "In my house, it used to be a joke that you couldn't live there unless you had a walker." Peps's mom lived for another 14 months with Peps and Vicky before passing away in 2002. As of this writing, in the summer of 2024, Vicky is still there.

"She was open to that, and I guess I took advantage of that," Vicky said, laughing. "So she's been my caregiver ever since then. She's given up the last 23 years to do my shopping and laundry, and you know [no one] else would do that but a real close friend."

From Peps's perspective, it was Vicky doing her the favor. "I loved taking care of my mom, doing her things, going and taking her to the doctor and all that," Peps said. "So I think that this was one of God's plans, that I could feel important taking care of somebody without changing my life too much, to still have my life. And it doesn't hurt to have another person or another cat in the house."

The division of labor is such that Vicky can dress herself and handle many of those basic tasks. But shopping, or doctor's visits, that's where Peps comes in. And there are plenty of the latter. But the two of them have never talked about it, about the enormous sacrifice and ways their lives changed forever that night on the highway. "I guess I probably take it for granted and don't talk about it too much," Vicky said. "But she's been through all my surgeries and aches and pains. I always have neuropathy, which is burning, and that never goes away. But I mean, there've been many times when I've had to lean on her to, you know, do some of my daily stuff."

The big-picture stuff also fell to Peps, who took over the framing business, while the two of them continued teaming up on the carnival circuit during the summer. The duo had plenty in common, Peps said, from a love of basketball to a preference for mild food. So to get out of the house, they began attending more games, once again connecting to the sport that had spawned their friendship and professional collaboration decades before.

Fortunately for them, a magical young point guard had just emerged for the University of Minnesota who held Peps and Vicky—and countless others—spellbound. The Lindsay Whalen era had arrived.

CHAPTER 5

LINDSAY

———

BEFORE THE WOMEN who have come to shape women's basketball over the past 60 years ever got the chance to do so, it is incredible to consider how many small circumstances *shaped them*, brought them into the orbit of this sport. Emil Neuman built a basketball hoop on the side of his barn and Peps found a lifelong calling. Dawn Shilling explained that there was more scholarship money in basketball than softball and Cheryl Reeve changed course.

And Lindsay Whalen? If there'd been girls' hockey where she grew up—in Hutchinson, Minnesota—the greatest player in University of Minnesota women's basketball history might never have picked up a basketball. Which stands to reason, because her father, Neil, played goalie for a Grand Forks High School team in North Dakota that won a pair of state titles, and her grandfather had season tickets to University of North Dakota hockey. So her mother, Kathy, put Lindsay in Girl Scouts, figure skating, and dance, but Lindsay said she could tell pretty early on how much she preferred going instead to events such as the Minnesota boys' high school state hockey tournament with her dad every year—yes, for the day off school and the doughnuts at the arena, but for the hockey too.

Lindsay wanted to do more than watch; she wanted to play. "My parents let me play when I was five, six years old," Whalen told me during an interview in 2022. "I convinced them that I wanted to play. Now, I was the only girl . . . there was no girls hockey. There [was] no varsity, middle school, bantams, whatever."

Whalen was talented, steadily moving up the chain of youth hockey—mites; squirt Bs, when Neil coached her; and on to Squirt As by fifth grade. "I was all in on hockey. I loved it," Whalen said. She never would have left. Friday and Saturday nights belonged to the University of Minnesota Gophers hockey team for the Whalens; Lindsay and her dad never missed a game. But when it came to Lindsay's path, her parents had other concerns. "They knew in hockey, there were no girls," Whalen said. "So who was my friend group going to be?"

Her best friend, Emily Inglis (now Heitz) played basketball, and Emily's dad, Tom, was the coach. So in the sixth grade Whalen decided to give it a try. She took the floor in Litchfield, Minnesota, and got the ball passed to her early in the game. She was not standing in an opportune place—the baseline, her angle such that she was behind the backboard. She rose and fired anyway—she was used to odd angles, from the way the gravel driveway behind her house sloped downward toward the family hoop. *Swish.* "The way the crowd responded, I knew that probably not many of the girls [would have] made that shot," Whalen said. "So I instantly was just hooked. And then I just kind of lived for the *oohs* and *aahs* of the fans."

There'd be plenty more of those. Whalen scored eight points that day, and quickly found that she would have a friend group in basketball, heading to Dairy Queen or Pizza Hut after Friday night games together, something that "was really healthy for me," Whalen joked.

But the basketball? Well, Whalen was a prodigy. Just a year after her debut, in seventh grade, she was moved up to the ninth-grade team. And a funny thing happened as the year went on. "Normally your ninth-grade basketball games: moms, dads, grandparents. That's it. Nobody there," her high school basketball coach, Andy Rostberg, told Sloane Martin back in 2018. "But about halfway through the year, more and more people were coming to watch the ninth-grade games because there was this little girl with a ponytail on top of her head running around and wowing people." People were watching ninth-grade girls' basketball because of Lindsay Whalen.

By eighth grade she was playing for both the ninth-grade and JV teams, getting time to learn with varsity as well. She remembers long nights of basketball, playing or cheering, from just after school at 4:00 PM until 9:00 PM. She got to know everyone, she said. "It was the greatest year of my life," Whalen said. "I became friends with everybody, developed this friend group. The tenth graders, they [could] see I could play, get them the ball in good spots. So they took me under their wing because I would make plays and score and we would be successful, and I would have been part of it."

By her freshman year of high school, the legend of Whalen had grown sufficiently that Hutchinson High School girls basketball games were standing-room-only events. Her first trip down the floor as a varsity player, she sank a three-pointer from the top of the key. She made Honorable Mention for the Star Tribune State Player of the

Year award that season, 1996–97, and in 1997–98 she led the Tigers to 23 straight wins.

But it was more than just the scoring numbers that turned Whalen into a must-see show in town. "It's hard to describe the impact she had back in 2000, 2001, 2002 when the state went crazy for girls' basketball," former Hutchinson girls' basketball coach Tim Ellefson said back in 2018. "She changed opinions about girls' abilities. Not only did she change the men, she changed the little girls. Now the little girls [were] thinking, *I can do more than just dribble with my right hand. I can go behind my back, I can spin. I can do what the boys do.*"

This was a personal challenge Whalen said she took on as well. When she'd face members of the boys' team in open gym, "I held my own or I beat them," she said. When it came time to see how big the crowds were, she "wanted to outdraw them."

And she did—not with social media but mere word of mouth. Older Hutchinson residents gathered at breakfast to share the exploits they'd seen, bringing their friends back with them, a whole town electrified. But even with all her heroics, she never did earn first-team All-State honors. She wasn't Minnesota's Ms. Basketball. In stories of her senior season, she's often mentioned as one among several U of M basketball commits, and not first. Even U of M didn't get around to recruiting her until after she began playing Amateur Athletic Union (AAU) ball her junior year, and that merely made her a regional target—Wisconsin, Iowa—and not a national phenomenon. The imagination of women's basketball wasn't quite big enough for Lindsay Whalen's talent. Not yet. These kinds of slights, they were critical in Whalen's eyes to both what she became and something she'd eventually look for when searching for talent herself. "Kids like that, they have so much to prove," Whalen said. "They're like, 'Okay, now I got this chance. What am I gonna do with this opportunity?'"

For Whalen, though, there was only one school for her: the University of Minnesota. She took a recruiting trip to Iowa and asked a simple question: "Do you get the Vikings games on TV?" Nope, Bears games, came the answer. By the time Lindsay got back into the car with her parents, she knew she wasn't going to the University of Iowa. Other schools tried to entice her by showing off their party scenes. But that wasn't for Lindsay Whalen. At all. She just wanted to go to school, hoop, and beat everyone in sight. And the oldest of five siblings, she knew sticking around at home meant getting to watch Katie, Casey, Annie, and Thomas grow up.

She even knew what the whole basketball experience should look and feel like, since she'd seen and heard what Williams Arena became during the 1996–97 season for the Minnesota men's basketball team, which featured five future NBA players, including Bobby Jackson and Sam Jacobson. That team regularly sold out Williams Arena, and the Gophers reached the Final Four. Whalen dedicated an entire wall of her bedroom to newspaper stories about that team. "They filled the whole Williams Arena with the celebration for them when they reached the Final Four," Whalen said. "And I remember being like, 'Oh, that'd be really cool.' But at that point, I didn't have a scholarship offer."

Fast-forward to Whalen's 2000–01 freshman season at the University of Minnesota, and her head coach, Cheryl Littlejohn, didn't have Final Four aspirations. She was just hoping, in year four of a five-year contract, to show some progress. And she turned the ball over to Whalen, making her the point guard from day one, a debut with 15 points and 7 rebounds against Binghamton.

The goal, as stated by Littlejohn, was .500 in the Big Ten. The reality was 1–15 in the Big Ten, a first-round loss to Indiana in the Big Ten Tournament, and Littlejohn's exit, though that had more to do with off-the-court problems than anything that happened in the win-loss columns (more on that later). Incidentally, any illusions that Whalen wouldn't be a star in college were shattered by the time Minnesota earned that single Big Ten win, with Lindsay scoring 31 on 14-for-17 from the field, adding 6 assists and 5 steals. She scored in double figures in every single game of her freshman season until February 18, 2001, just missing the mark that day with nine points and putting on the kind of shows that had thrilled capacity crowds in Hutchinson.

And while the Final Four seemed like a pipe dream that freshman season, filling Williams Arena would have been literally impossible for Whalen to accomplish, even if she'd scored 60 points a night and the Gophers went undefeated. Because while the men played at the iconic arena affectionately known as the Barn, the women played at the Sports Pavilion, without anything close to the same atmosphere and with about a third of the seating capacity.

It is the easy counterargument to simply point out that the Gophers women's basketball team, as of February 22 of that season, had averaged just 1,055 fans per game, and to say that the administration was doing them a favor playing them in the Pavilion—after all, that small of a crowd would have been positively microscopic in the Barn. But this is the lazy argument used time and again regarding women's sports, an attempt to minimize them using outcomes while failing to examine the inputs. Sending every signal that a women's team matters less—to the point of playing their games in a lesser arena—affects the choices people make about whether or not to attend. It impacts the team's play itself.

Things got even uglier after the 2000–01 season. Even though in late February 2001, the *Star Tribune* reported Littlejohn's job was safe, that was prior to her being accused of paying players and asking some players to lie in school inquiries during the ensuing investigation. The school was perfectly comfortable with the results, but the scandal was a different matter, and Littlejohn was fired in May 2001. Obvious candidates to replace Littlejohn—such as Bonnie Henrickson, a Willmar, Minnesota, native and head coach at Virginia Tech—declined to even be considered. Henrickson, a St. Cloud State graduate, chose the Big East over the Big Ten, though she eventually took the job a few years later at Kansas. So this wasn't about Virginia Tech; it was about Minnesota.

Once again, the gap between treatment of the men's and women's programs was laid bare. Littlejohn earned just $101,500. But as the *Star Tribune* reported, the conversation within the administration wasn't about how much more they would be spending on a new coach to find more success for the program but whether they'd spend even that much on the new coach. "The institution is not in a position to put any new money in to cover this," university vice president Tonya Moten Brown said on May 24, 2001. "Obviously we're in a serious position as to our budget." Conversely, the men's coach, Dan Monson, earned $490,000 in 2000–01. And Minnesota had paid former men's coach Clem Haskins a $1.5 million buyout over allegations of academic fraud in his program back in 1999.

Ultimately the school came up to $130,000, plus incentives that could push the package to around $200,000—or 40 percent of Monson's annual haul—to bring in midwesterner Brenda Oldfield (now Frese) as the new women's head coach. She'd led a huge turnaround in her previous stop at Ball State—from 9–17 before she arrived to 16–13, then 19–9 in her two seasons in Muncie. She made no promises that it would be the same at U of M, though. "I don't think it's until your third year [when] you're going to be able to see significant change," she told the *Star Tribune* in June 2001. But she was wrong, even though two critical parts of the recruiting class that came in with Whalen—forward Megan Kane and guard/forward Tanisha Gilbert— left the team and underwent surgery for an ACL tear, respectively.

Despite keeping expectations low—.500 was where she set the bar—Brenda saw the true change necessary for the program no less than Whalen did. "Once we sell out the Pavilion—which is 5,600—on a consistent basis, we are moving to Williams Arena," Brenda said. Destiny, however, would take a hand.

Despite being picked to finish eighth in the Big Ten (with 11 teams at the time, now 14, and 18 by 2025—long story), the Gophers roared out to a fast start. It took 49 points from Kelly Mazzante to lift Penn State over Minnesota in their Big Ten opener, but Minnesota beat Michigan State 70–69 on a game-winning layup from Whalen. On January 20, 2002, Whalen walked into a sold-out Kohl Center, scored 32 points, and ended Wisconsin's 15-game winning streak 92–85. "It's a player's dream to play in front of a sold-out crowd like this," Whalen said that afternoon.

That win got Minnesota into the top 25. You might think that would be enough to push Minnesota to move its women's basketball games to Williams Arena, to show off the elite team headlined by a flashy in-state point guard. But it didn't. Instead, it took a broken water pipe.

Early Saturday morning, January 19, 2002, a three-inch sprinkler pipe broke open, and hundreds of gallons of water spilled onto the Sports Pavilion floor. While the athletic department managed to get the water pumped out in time to host a gymnastics meet at the Pavilion that evening, by the next day the floor had begun to buckle, and clearly needed to be replaced.

The women's team hadn't played in Williams Arena since 1993 (when renovations to the Sports Pavilion forced the university to let them play there), and the lead-up to the game against Indiana carried no hint of what was to come. Oldfield spoke about the loss of the home court as "unfortunate." *Star Tribune* columnist C.J. urged people who "don't care about today's NFL conference title games" to pack the arena. (There were plenty of those people in the area—the Vikings finished 6–10 that year and missed the playoffs entirely.)

Would it surprise you to know that back in 1993, when the women's team played at Williams, they'd set the attendance record for the program at 6,746? It was a number higher than the seating capacity at the Pavilion. And yet, at the first opportunity back then, the team was ushered back into the smaller Sports Pavilion, even though the Gophers that year were ranked in the Top 25.

It was a double standard that had weighed on Whalen, even as she felt powerless to do anything about it. "I wanted [our team to fill Williams]," Whalen said. "But you're just trying to survive. To make sure you get to class on time. I was trying to get my assignments done, to get a good GPA, because I wasn't the best student in high school." Whalen, in other words, had the crazy notion that a full-time student course load at U of M, while doing things on the basketball court no other player had done before, should have been enough. And that Sunday, given the opportunity of fate, it turned out to be more than enough.

Coach Oldfield held her team in the locker room ahead of that Sunday game against Indiana for a very important reason: the crowd was still filing in. Williams Arena was not prepared for what was about to hit it. They hadn't adequately staffed for it. And so the game was delayed 10, 15, 20 minutes. And inside their locker room, tucked away from it, Whalen and her teammates could still hear this buildup of sound like they'd never heard before on campus.

The plan was to simply open the lower level of seats at the Barn. The lines stretching around the arena to see Whalen and the Gophers quickly changed that plan. The upper level was hastily deployed a half hour before scheduled tip-off.

Officials from the arena told Brenda to wait, then to wait again. Her team had warmed up. Finally, they were given the green light. Lindsay and her teammates ran down the tunnel, out onto the Williams Arena court, and were enveloped by the sound. Whalen, in that moment, flashed back to moments from her freshman season at the Pavilion, when around 500 people would be in the stands. "And [I was] like, 'This is insane,'" she remembered saying to her teammates. "Like, to watch us. And to come from where we were the year before."

The day itself was a study in that ever-present combination of celebration over progress and astonishment at how long it took and how far there remained to go. When everyone had been admitted, 11,389 people packed Williams Arena. It mirrored the nearly 12,000 who had showed up for the very first game at the Barn, when men were given the opportunity to play there in February 1928. "The record-breaking crowd of 12,000 [was] kept in a frenzy by the frequent shifting of the lead," the *Lima Morning Star and Republican-Gazette* breathlessly reported on February 5, 1928. It took 74 years for the women to get the same treatment.

Vendors ran out of T-shirts. "We were expecting about 5,000 people," a manager at the arena explained. WCCO-AM 830 ran a radio broadcast of the game, the first of the season. Why did it take until then to begin radio broadcasts of the women's basketball team?

It turned out that building a great product and then selling it was all it took, just as it did in the men's game. As *Star Tribune* columnist Brian Wicker put it the next day, "Previous efforts of drumming up such support [for the women's team] smacked of charity work." No magic trick required. As Carley Knox, a figure who brought this ethos to the Minnesota Lynx (and who will soon feature in this book) would put it: "If you don't value your own product, no one else will."

What does that mean, exactly? University of Minnesota president Mark Yudof said to a booster, as he took in the crowd: "If I had known we could have done this, I would have broken the pipe myself a lot earlier." That Yudof and the Minnesota decision-makers could have done this without an act of God and plumbing didn't seem to have occurred to him.

Of course, given the audience she'd envisioned years earlier, Whalen put on a show. She scored 22 points, 18 of them in a second-half surge that turned a tie game with 4:45 left into a comfortable 75–60 win; added five rebounds and five assists; and earned this praise from

Indiana head coach Kathi Bennett: "Lindsay Whalen is the best point guard in the Big Ten Conference."

Oldfield, seeing her prophecy come true ahead of schedule, was already looking to what came next: "It was awesome that we could take our game to more than 5,700 people. . . . Now, I hope they'll want to return."

Hundreds stuck around to get their new Gophers apparel autographed by Whalen and her teammates. "We all have T-shirts and we're ready to come back to the next game," Cathy Sigvertsen of St. Paul told the *Star Tribune* that afternoon. She'd been a men's season-ticket holder. Now she was all in for the women's team.

The Minnesota women's basketball team played its home games at Williams Arena for the rest of the season. And ever since. Lindsay Whalen had changed the course of the sport again. "At that point, like since that game, the trajectory of it—I mean, they had to build a conference room and a players' lounge and a women's locker room, a video room at Williams Arena," Whalen said, taking stock of it all. "Because the women's basketball team then played in there from that point on."

Whalen said it hits her every once in a while, the impact her presence that day had on so much that has come since. "There are times you think, *Oh, that was crazy*," she said. "It's changing infrastructure to build the change. And that's where we're at."

That attendance record of 11,389 lasted less than a month. The Gophers women drew 12,142 against Michigan State on February 24, 2002. The team's *total* season attendance the year before? Just 11,957. "The whole thing just kind of exploded," Whalen said. "You'd go and talk with your parents, and everybody's there. And it was like, 'Wow, we really did something.'"

As Patrick Reusse wrote in the *Star Tribune* the day after the game: "As it turned out, the Pavilion flood was the best thing that ever happened to women's basketball at Minnesota." But without Whalen? The flood wouldn't have accomplished anything. Columnist Sid Hartman reported that February that Oldfield had already requested to Yudof that Williams Arena be the team's home court. Put another way, a cinematic day like the one the Gophers fashioned—the pipe bursting itself—wasn't enough for the administration. Further lobbying was necessary for the Gophers to keep their new home, despite the dramatic attendance surge.

Whalen's Gophers finished 22–8 and reached the NCAA tournament as a five seed, beating UNLV before falling to fourth seed and host North Carolina in the second round. Whalen won Big Ten Player of the Year, Oldfield won Big Ten Coach of the Year, and Gophers center Janel McCarville won Freshman of the Year. Minnesota won 11 Big Ten games and finished not the predicted eighth but second. Whalen earned the cover of the sports section of the *Star Tribune* again and again. She was no longer Hutchinson's secret star.

But the following season, she'd have to do it without Oldfield. The coach had been vocal about wanting more support from the administration for the program, and her salary ranked among the lowest of Big Ten coaches. After a turnaround no one thought possible, other programs came calling, and Oldfield was blunt about hearing them out. The University of Maryland offered her a raise that more than doubled her salary to $275,000 per year. The Maryland Terrapins had built a new arena, the Xfinity Center, which was scheduled to open the following August. Still unknown was what the NCAA would impose on Minnesota in terms of sanctions for the rules violations committed by Oldfield's predecessor, Cheryl Littlejohn. Oldfield accepted Maryland's offer.

Whalen understands it now, of course, but was crushed at the time. She found out about it on the very first cell phone she ever owned—after convincing her dad to let her have a Nokia, you know, "for safety." And while she was in the crowd watching the 2002 Final Four, she heard from somebody via text: "Your coach is leaving." She didn't believe it, but more and more texts came, Lindsay answering them slowly, T9-style, the reality gradually becoming clear.

The next morning, she returned to University Village, where the team all lived. She and her teammates sat with Oldfield as the coach spoke with them through tears for 35 minutes. Whalen spoke to a reporter at the *Star Tribune* when it was over that day in early April, musing aloud about loyalty. "We're finding out the hard way that there's not much," she said. That there are many who hold a grudge against the coach to this day in Minnesota is an understatement. But what's happened in the 20-plus years since largely vindicates Oldfield's decision.

Reportedly, one of the reasons Oldfield gave to Minnesota at the time of her departure was that she thought the recruiting base was stronger in the DMV (Delaware-Maryland-Virginia) area. Whalen took that as a personal challenge. "I just took that as, 'Well, we're going to go win here,'" Whalen recalled. "Everyone was like, 'No, we're not going anywhere. We're staying put.'" Oldfield directly denied that, and her version of events was later seconded by Minnesota vice president Tonya Moten Brown. But the early reports stuck in the public consciousness.

It didn't help that hiring Oldfield's replacement proved to be such a debacle. This was in part due to the investigation by the NCAA over Littlejohn's transgressions, which stretched on as the NCAA's actions so often do. And it was also in part because the school's plans to merge its women's and men's athletic departments meant that the women's teams would have to make do with less thanks to the payout to Haskins, the former men's coach.

Cheryl Burnett, Reeve's old adversary in the Missouri Valley Conference (MVC), was interviewed for the job but turned it down. Reeve's mentor Joe McKeown also expressed interest, and his family had a house in Brainerd, Minnesota, but the Gophers couldn't get him to leave George Washington. Pam Tanner, head coach at the University of Denver, chose to remain in her job instead of moving from the Sun Belt Conference to the Big Ten. Minneapolis North High School coach Faith Johnson Patterson was urged to pursue the job by friends but never even applied. Liz Podominick, then a junior in high school and a top 20 recruit nationally, put it simply to the *Star Tribune*: "It's chaos over there, and it's frustrating. They're going lower and lower on my list every day."

Ultimately the Gophers hired Pam Borton, who'd been an assistant at Boston College, and prior to that, a head coach at Vermont. They paid her $150,000 as a base salary. Incentives were tied to things such as attendance at Williams Arena. An article in the *Star Tribune* at the time of Borton's hiring noted that Minnesota could help solve its athletic department's financial woes by not only continuing to play women's games at Williams Arena but stopping the practice of ticket giveaways for the in-demand product. As Dara Worrell, an athletics administrator at the University of Tennessee, put it: "People are going to come to these games. Why should we cheapen the ticket?" In case you wondered, Pat Summitt's UT program led the nation in average attendance that season, at 14,295 fans per game. But getting Minnesota to Tennessee's level wasn't the task in front of Borton. First, she had to prove she was even up to the job.

"I realize there were other people in front of me, but their concerns have created this opportunity," Borton said at her introductory news conference, held at Williams Arena, in May 2002. "I'm sure there were 100 applicants for this job. If I'm the third or fourth one they wanted, that's great. It doesn't bother me at all."

She'd also passed muster with Whalen, who was on the hiring committee. "Pam had to come in, instill some discipline," Whalen said, looking back. "And that's why we went to the Final Four."

Borton, incidentally, even signed Podominick. The Gophers went 25–6 in Whalen's junior year, climbing as high as ninth in the Associated Press poll and reaching the NCAA Sweet 16, defeating Stanford and head coach Tara VanDerveer 68–56 on the road at Maples Pavilion to do so. The Gophers lost to Texas in the Sweet 16, denying Whalen a chance to face LSU and future Lynx teammate Seimone Augustus in a regional final, but entered Whalen's senior season a legitimate candidate to win the national title.

Whalen was a first-team All-American preseason. Minnesota began the season 13th in the AP poll and raced out to a 15–0 start. Whalen's No. 13 jerseys were everywhere. The school even began selling bobbleheads of Whalen. Attendance swelled at Williams Arena. Whalen broke two bones in her shooting hand in a game against Ohio State, but it didn't stop her—she returned after five weeks somehow playing through it for the rest of the season.

By NCAA tournament time, the Gophers were hosting, and 12,257 people watched Whalen score 31 in a first-round win over UCLA. And 13,425 saw Whalen finish just shy of a triple-double in a second-round win over Kansas State. The Gophers beat Pam Borton's old team, Boston College, in the Sweet 16 and then faced the powerhouse from Duke, led by Alana Beard, the top seed in the region and winners of 13 straight. It didn't matter. Lindsay Whalen would not be denied. With 27 points from Whalen, and 20 points and 18 rebounds from McCarville, the Gophers had reached the goal Whalen had envisioned when she arrived on a team with eight Big Ten wins over its previous five seasons, playing in a secondary, forgotten gym: the Final Four, where she and her team would show everyone what Williams Arena could look, sound, and feel like for a women's team. In the final minute of the Duke game, Whalen thrust both hands into the air to celebrate victory, her team bound for New Orleans.

By the time she arrived in New Orleans, Whalen was reflective about how much she had overcome—all the turmoil pushed aside like a defender running into Whalen's shoulder on a drive. Did she ever doubt she'd be there? At a press conference ahead of the national semifinals, she said:

> That's tough to say. I think that I obviously watched the Final Fours the past years, and I've been down here at the Final Four, and you always dream, you always hope, and you always think that you start every year as a goal to make it to the Final Four. But obviously this year I think a month and a half ago or whenever I was injured—and we had a little rough stretch in the middle of the season—we still held out hope, but things weren't looking that great. And for us

to make this run is just incredible, and it's a tribute to our team . . . and you got to give everyone credit for staying confident and staying with this goal. It was the goal at the beginning of the year, and I think the coaches reiterated that when we went out, when we had a tough stretch, that this still was our goal. And for us to accomplish that is a great goal, and we're obviously not done yet.

It was a team with 10 players—*10*—from Minnesota. They all played high school basketball against one another in a system Peps Neuman worked to create. "I think that that's a big reason why I chose to come to Minnesota, is that you hear of all the names that have left the state and you see them playing—some of them in the WNBA, some of them like at Stanford and Georgia and all over the country," Whalen said. "You see great players leaving Minnesota. I think that we just needed to take one class or a couple of individuals to stay here and turn the program around, and then we would start to get your Shannon Bolden and your Shannon Schonrock, and . . . you can go down the line of all the players from Minnesota that have come here. And we'll take one Wisconsin player or two. We'll take a few imports. We're not biased."

The run came to an end against Connecticut in New Orleans, and Whalen's future longtime USA Basketball teammate Diana Taurasi. The two managed to hold one another to detente—Whalen shot 3-for-11, Taurasi 6-for-17—but Minnesota never overcame an early Huskies lead and fell 67–58.

That didn't really matter, though. Whalen had changed the definition of what Minnesota women's basketball could, even *should*, look like. An entire state figured out that Williams Arena wasn't just a home for the women's basketball Gophers but for all of them too. That included Peps Neuman and Vicky Nelson, who began attending Minnesota women's basketball games at the Barn during Lindsay Whalen's sophomore season. By her senior year, they were season ticket holders, and they have been ever since. Peps and Vicky even found the silver lining in Vicky's accident. "When we started going to Williams Arena, we were very lucky Vicky was in a wheelchair," Peps said, the two of them laughing. "Because that seating, it's right in the front row. So there's one advantage to being in the wheelchair: we get to sit in the front row."

Eventually Peps would become almost as critical a part of the Williams Arena experience as the team itself. During the 2006–07 season, a few fans in Peps and Vicky's section noticed that Vicky always put her jacket over her legs—she'd get cold at the games. In an effort to make her more comfortable, they bought her a beautiful maroon-and-gold University of Minnesota blanket. Peps lifted it to show to the crowd in gratitude, and they applauded. Never one to disappoint an audience, Peps brought the blanket along to the next section, and they applauded too.

It grew from there, until "[eventually] I got to where I run all the way down and back up the sideline," Peps said with a chuckle. Within a few years, the Minnesota pep band had christened her the Blanket Lady. Every single game Peps and Vicky attend—and that's virtually every home game—Peps gets massive cheers, running with her blanket up and down the sideline during a third-quarter timeout. She carefully looks for the right moment, one that won't take focus from the game, and entertains the fans like she did in the early 1960s.

She doesn't get paid by the school, or even get free tickets for it, and that suits her just fine—"If they gave me free tickets, I'd feel like it is a job," she said.

A few weeks after her team was eliminated from the tournament, Lindsay Whalen watched the 2004 WNBA Draft on her television. The Minnesota Lynx, 12th in the WNBA in attendance in 2003, had the sixth overall pick. Diana Taurasi went first to Phoenix, Alana Beard second to Washington, Nicole Powell third to the Charlotte Sting. The Connecticut Sun had the next selection, and they offered it to the Lynx—in exchange for Minnesota's two first-round picks, 6 and 7, along with two starters, one of them the great Katie Smith. The Lynx turned them down. It generated days of negative coverage in the state. For instance, in response to Lynx executive Roger Griffith expressing the hope that fans would be "savvy enough" to understand why they wouldn't accept such an offer, Brian Wicker wrote in the *Star Tribune*: "We're savvy enough to understand this: the Lynx just passed, however steep the cost, on their best chance to change the summer habits of a lot of Minnesotans."

With that, Sun coach Mike Thibault had his point guard in Connecticut, and Whalen would have to wait to play for the other point guard in the 1988 NCAA tournament game between Penn State and La Salle who went on to coach the Minnesota Lynx (namely, Cheryl Reeve). "That was tough," Whalen recalled in 2022. "Yeah, that was tough. That was the first time and I'm the oldest of five, who [were all] really still at home. But it was great for me. So I had to grow up. You know, I had to learn how to figure some things out on my own. Like how to go get your own bank account. Figure out different things. And Mike Thibault was like a second dad to me."

The Lynx had finished 18–16 in 2003. In 2004 they finished 18–16 again. Attendance stayed flat. Meanwhile, Thibault and Whalen made the 2004 WNBA Finals. That didn't exactly reassure anybody that the Lynx had made the right call.

What Lindsay Whalen meant to Minnesota was never in dispute. How Minnesota institutions can build on what Lindsay Whalen started is an active, multipart debate across youth, college, and professional basketball.

The Gophers have never reached the heights of that Lindsay Whalen 2004 season since, even when figures such as Rachel Banham have developed in the youth system pioneered by Peps Neuman and Vicky Nelson and revolutionized by Whalen's elevation of the ceiling. And for the Lynx to do more than simply win on the court—to be a profitable, sustainable business that made women's basketball a given in Minnesota, it would take the collective efforts of Whalen, of Reeve, and of a visionary businesswoman who came to understand from her own hard-won, personal battles that such a team must be fully inclusive, and unapologetically themselves. But first, Carley Knox had to get thrown out of a few places while she rattled some cages.

CHAPTER 6

CARLEY AND CHERYL

I**N ORDER TO EVEN BE** in the position to change women's basketball, Cheryl Reeve needed to be diverted from the softball diamond. Lindsay Whalen was redirected away from the hockey rink. And so it was too with Carley Knox and the soccer field, her first sports love and a sport she still speaks about with the passion of a calling, even after so many years redefining the way the sport of women's basketball is marketed, consumed, and valued.

Knox wrote back in 2004:

> The "beautiful game" entered my life when I was about four as I began to sneak into my older brother's soccer practices. My father was his coach, and I refused to sit idly on the sidelines picking daisies. Because the sport intrigued me, I soon began sneaking into drills, which eventually led to invitations to join every practice, as my father must have sensed a spark of potential. Community soccer ushered me into club soccer, club soccer evolved into high school and

Olympic Development soccer, and high school and club soccer turned into an opportunity to play Division I collegiate
soccer. Along the way, my father coached almost every team
on which I played until college. My father remains my biggest supporter, probably one of my closest friends to this
day, and someone who still challenges me.

The world as it related to women athletes was a very different
place during Carley Knox's childhood in the 1990s than it had been
for Peps Neuman or Cheryl Reeve. Much of what Peps and Cheryl
fought for were givens for Carley, who was born six years after
Title IX was signed. But in terms of Carley's athletic progress, the
family and the town that surrounded her fostered her talents more
than any law ever could.

Carley told me in a 2018 interview:

I'm from Toledo, Ohio, originally and I grew up playing
every sport you can think of, including playing football with
full pads with the boys all the way through to middle school.
And then I went to an all-girls Catholic high school. I was
really blessed to have two parents who were incredibly supportive and a really enlightened father in terms of he thought
it was always important to have strong, powerful female role
models in my life, and the same with my mother.

We would have season tickets to University of Toledo
women's basketball. We would go all the time, and back
in the day of Dana Drew and Denise Pickenpaugh, when
[now–Iowa State head coach] Bill Fennelly was there, [and
it] was really fun to grow up and see them and have them
as role models.

For Carley, the coach of most of her soccer teams growing up was her father, Chris, and though she excelled on the field, she maintained a dream more Jill Ellis than Crystal Dunn—she wanted to be a soccer coach. It's the answer she gave to people when she was as young as six years old and they'd ask what she wanted to be when she grew up. "I want to be a women's soccer coach," she would say. The vision was clear. "My desired career path was inspired by observing my father and other similar coaches who changed lives, made their players better athletes, and helped their players become the best people they could possibly be on and off the field," Knox wrote in 2004. "Maybe the coaching bug has always been a part of me in that I have always wanted to positively impact people's lives, to make a difference, and in the process to create better soccer players."

Chris always had multiple women on his staff, Carley remembered, and the idea of becoming a strong, empowered woman was entirely tied to her identity as a soccer player in her view. Moreover, an infrastructure existed. Carley Knox wanted to be a soccer player, and at every level, the opportunities abounded. Community soccer became club soccer, which became high school soccer, Olympic development soccer, and ultimately the opportunity to play the sport at a Division I school.

Chris and Anna had always emphasized to Carley that she could do anything. She excelled at soccer and in school, and had her pick of colleges, considering West Point and others before settling upon Ohio University, which had everything she could ask for academically, from sports administration to sports sociology, and a group of fellow young recruits and returning talent she could sense was on the cusp of massive success on the field. She'd be a three-and-a-half-hour drive from home, close enough to visit but far enough to build her own identity.

That last part mattered more to Carley than many other young college students, as her long-maintained external sense of self came up against the ways in which she discovered she truly wished to live—as an out lesbian but also as someone who needed to find more emotional capacity generally to live as her authentic self in every way. "When I entered college, I further explored this notion of empowerment and came to resist identities which I felt pressured to maintain while in high school: standout [soccer] athlete, scholar, heterosexual, and the perfect daughter," Knox recalled. "Although it was once my primary aim to please my parents, my school, and society by maintaining these multiple identities, I began to question a piece of that image that often felt forced, uncomfortable, and just not me."

When she struck up a friendship with a woman on another team, some of her teammates warned her she should be "careful" around her.

But that's not how Carley Knox approached life. She wrote:

> However, instead of being wary of possible "corruption," my curiosity was piqued, and I was subsequently introduced to the lesbian student-athlete community within our athletic department. Thus, it was while establishing a relationship with another female athlete that I came to terms with my sexuality. It was at this time that the rules of being a lesbian student-athlete were brought to my attention by my peers through such admonitions as: "Be careful who you tell." "Don't shove it in peoples' faces." "Silence is the safest way." "Don't get involved with the gay groups on campus . . . they are scary."

"At all costs protect yourself and your scholarship." As I was issued the rules of engagement, I felt disheartened in that for the first time I felt truly alive but was once again warned of constraints by societal expectations.

The very lessons that Cheryl had internalized were being forced on Carley for the very first time. But interestingly, she didn't sublimate her newfound sense of self. She redirected her academic life around it. Her new major? Sports industry and women's studies, with a minor in coaching. She said:

As I evolved into an out lesbian and a die-hard feminist, I was able to complement my academic and athletic endeavors by becoming a diversity educator and a political activist. Despite my peers' warnings, I got involved with activist groups such as Feminist Majority, Open Doors, and Swarm of Dykes, while also bridging a long-standing gap between the lesbian activist groups and the lesbian student-athlete community. Through my participation in these groups, I developed grandiose dreams of changing the world and became even more dedicated to educating wherever I went. I felt as if this new intellectual passion and this new activist passion were filling a void in my life I had never recognized, a void that could never be filled by athletics alone. Whether I was programming about diversity awareness within the athletic department, educating a new teammate about confronting homophobia, or protesting discrimination or hate crimes, I never hid this aspect of my life. Rather, I dedicated what little free time I had to help create a more open athletic department environment and to fight homophobia in general. GLBT activism and feminism shaped my life just as much as my involvement in soccer.

The doors that approach opened for her, along with the doors it closed, would shape the rest of her professional life. And perhaps even more important to the world was Knox's awakening of intersectionality: "As I came to terms with my sexuality, I began to realize not only the oppression of women as well as the oppression of the gay, lesbian, bisexual, and transgender (GLBT) community but discrimination that all marginalized groups face." That this served as a guiding light for organizations she'd work for, and eventually lead, would lead to dizzyingly vital consequences for social justice fights to come.

First, though, came the end of her soccer playing days. Her instincts were correct: Ohio was about to become a force, even a contender for a Mid-American Conference (MAC) championship, with Knox scoring a critical goal in the final five seconds of an overtime to force a second overtime in an eventual loss to Northern Illinois in the MAC Conference title game in 1998.

So as her collegiate career came to a close, Knox faced the very same abrupt ending that Karen Healey, Kim Franchi, Lisa Angelotti, and so many others had faced in the Title IX era. She had a standout college soccer career, and played at a talent level that in today's game would have meant professional opportunities here in America. (As it stood, Carley was only offered a chance to play in Germany.) The Women's United Soccer Association (WUSA) existed, but the league had already spent five years of funding in its first season, and folded by the fall of 2003. Knox said:

> Where do you go from here? You're playing the best soccer of your life, and what are you to do? My opportunity was to either go play professionally in Germany or start my

coaching career. I was playing the best soccer of my life, and all of a sudden it just stopped dead. That's a traumatic thing. You've done something your entire life year-round and dedicated your life to it. Obviously, it paid you back in paying for college and having a great experience there, but at the same time you're just living it and breathing it 24/7, and then you play your last game and you're like, "Wait, it's over?"

But Knox had prepared for this moment, with the ambition she'd held since the age of six—coaching women's soccer—foremost in her mind. Nor was this a mere pipe dream on her part; she'd done the work. Knox wrote in 2004:

At the time of my graduation from Ohio University, I had prepared myself along the way by coaching soccer for approximately eight years. I came to believe that coaching was my "true calling" and that no other profession could match the passion I had for commanding a soccer field. My dream of one day playing for the U.S. Women's National Soccer Team evolved into a dream of one day coaching the U.S. Women's National [Soccer] Team. I coached several club teams, a multitude of college and private camps all over the United States, clinics for high schools and groups of collegiate-bound women soccer players, and individual players just looking to improve. Additionally, I attended the national Soccer Coaches Convention every year, consistently networked for future job opportunities with countless collegiate coaches, and received several of the résumé-boosting coaching licenses. With my solid playing career and years of coaching preparation, I was confident in my abilities to succeed at the Division I level and felt anxious to begin my collegiate coaching career. I was ready to begin the next chapter of my life.

So armed with a stellar playing career, peerless recommendations, a long list of credentials and experience, Carley Knox set off into the world of coaching confident nothing would stop her. She also had no intention of hiding her true self and was unapologetically out. As she told friends who warned her not to be so open about her life, "I want a program to hire me for me." But that proved far more difficult than she had anticipated.

She recalled:

In 2001 I began to communicate with a Top 25 coach, who happened to have recruited me out of high school and had become a family friend. Our communication eventually turned into a job offer, and I was elated at the prospect of working with this man and with [a program at] the caliber of his program. He made a verbal offer over the phone and I enthusiastically accepted. When I called him a week later, I was absolutely blown away to find he had changed his mind and had given the job to a woman I considered less qualified for the position. In fact, I played against this woman for four years and knew her personally. I had seen her résumé and felt that she did not have half the experiences I had acquired over the years. Reeling in shock, I called some of my coaching friends to decipher what exactly happened and how he could have done this to me. The responses I received varied from "You are too gay, Carley" to "Someone has been calling around informing

coaches of your sexuality." A mutual friend also informed
me that the coach did not believe his school was the place
for a lesbian coach.

Knox was crushed but undaunted. She took a job at a lesser program, one that had struggled in the same conference as the job she
thought she'd gotten. It was a small town, with no LGBTQ+ public
presence. Within the first few days there, she learned the women's
lacrosse coach had been fired shortly after coming out. The warning
was clear: don't do the same thing. She endured homophobic slurs
and jokes all year long in her lone season there.

So let's take a moment and consider the professional lives of Carley Knox and Cheryl Reeve, circa 2001–02. Because we live here, in
the future, we come to it with the understanding that these are two
of the most important figures in sports history, who ultimately transformed a franchise, a business model, and a sport itself. Both of them
did everything the right way professionally, excelling at each stop,
finding mentors along the way eager to help, and charting a course
along a path any successful man in coaching would recognize well.

They even serve as models of the scientific method as it relates
to how publicly to live as a lesbian at that time. Carley, the activist.
Cheryl, quietly determined to live her life without letting her sexuality
get in the way of her professional ambitions. "When I look back at
it, on the way that I lived, I'm so mad at myself," Cheryl said with
a chuckle. "To allow it. But it felt like [the price of admission] at
that time."

And yet as the 21st century dawned, neither one had very
much success holding down a regular job. "I have now come to the

disheartening realization that it is nearly impossible to 'be who I am' and become a Division I head collegiate coach," Knox wrote in 2004. "I have never been one to walk away from a challenge, but I have decided to take a break from a profession that threatens to compromise who I am as a person. This has allowed me to approach the frustrating situation from a different angle." She didn't think any differently in 2018, saying, "I would say the reason that I am not coaching women's soccer today is because of homophobia."

The two of them kept fighting, obviously, but found different avenues to do so. Knox went back to school, pursuing a master's in education at Bowling Green State University. Her 2004 writings in this book came from her thesis at BGSU: "Behind Closed Locker Room Doors: How Homophobia Operates in Collegiate Division I Women's Athletics."

Knox wrote:

> I have now focused my energies on doing research on what I experienced as the oppressive state of women's Division I collegiate athletics, in hopes of ultimately bringing about change as a scholar. Additionally, I now have a new long-term goal of becoming a Division I athletic director, which will hopefully provide another means of bettering women's athletics. Although I faced ostracism as a player and discrimination contributed to forcing me out of the collegiate coaching ranks, my on-field passion for soccer has turned into an academic passion to understand and conceptualize how to overcome this form of oppression. Still, the soccer field continues to pull me back, and my hope remains to find a position within a more open and inclusive athletic department.

She never did, but her study is vital to understanding the landscape. This wasn't a Carley Knox problem or a Cheryl Reeve problem. This was a widespread problem in collegiate athletics.

For Cheryl? The landscape in women's basketball offered something beyond the collegiate game. She'd gotten a close look at the WNBA as an Indiana Fever season ticket holder, and she knew something else too: fellow New Jersey product Anne Donovan was merely the interim coach with the Fever in 2000, until Nell Fortner returned from a hiatus coaching USA Basketball. After that stint, Donovan was a finalist for the Phoenix Mercury head coaching gig that eventually went to Cynthia Cooper-Dyke. But the Charlotte Sting hired Donovan to take over for T. R. Dunn in 2001, and Donovan needed some help on her staff.

The money was not the kind that could serve as a definitive answer to Cheryl's father's continued pleas to get her to use her computer science degree in another field besides coaching. "I remember Anne calling and saying, 'I have a specific position, but it's just a seasonal gig and it's for $5,000,'" Reeve said. "I was undeterred." The job came with an apartment, too.

Donovan knew she was getting a bargain. "You could see out of the gates what kind of coach Cheryl was going to be," she told me in 2017.

The stakes in Charlotte were considerably higher than just to make the team into a winner. The Sting had finished at the very bottom of the WNBA in average attendance in 2000, and ownership, always seemingly with one foot out the door, made it clear it considered the continued existence of the Sting a live question. "The pressure was to get the thing turned around so we could make sure we had a team," Reeve said in a phone interview in the summer of 2023. "Because we knew if we kept on losing, they weren't going to want to keep the team."

The impact of ownership's year-to-year approach affected even the first draft Donovan, Reeve, and lead assistant Trudi Lacey collaborated on in 2001. With the second overall pick, and a mandate to get better defensively—Dunn's 2000 Sting finished with a defensive rating of 106.0, one of the worst marks in WNBA history—the Sting could have selected Stratford, New Jersey's own Tamika Catchings out of Tennessee. But Catchings had suffered a torn ACL that January and wouldn't be able to play until 2002. Ownership wouldn't allow the Sting to select someone unless she could play right away. Charlotte selected guard Kelly Miller, who ended up playing three seasons with the team.

Consider it a parting gift from Reeve to her former season ticket-holding friends. Indiana selected Catchings third, and she went on to win five Defensive Player of the Year awards, amassing the most win shares of any player in WNBA history for the Indiana Fever.

The Sting began the season 1–10, despite early, solid work from veterans such as Andrea Stinson and Dawn Staley. At that point, at an event for season-ticket holders, Donovan guaranteed a playoff appearance. "It was ridiculous," Donovan said. "We had either never been to the playoffs or hadn't been there in a long time. Saying it to them, we were going to make the playoffs—and the players, all this goes back to those players, because Dawn and Andrea Stinson, Allison Feaster, Charlotte Smith, all of them instead of looking for a reason or somebody to blame or something to cry about, they just decided they were going to get it done."

The Sting got on a roll, finishing the season by winning 17 of their last 21 games, knocking off the heavily favored Cleveland

Rockers, coached by Dan Hughes, then beating the New York Liberty at Madison Square Garden to advance to the WNBA Finals, before falling to Lisa Leslie's Los Angeles Sparks. The crowds got bigger and bigger, ultimately leading to a 25.9 percent rise in attendance from the previous season. Donovan, Reeve, and Staley did what they were supposed to—brought a winner to Charlotte—and revenue trended up.

It didn't matter. George Shinn, who would cast a shadow over both the Hornets and Sting with his very public trial for sexual assault, ran out on the Sting just before the 2002 WNBA season began. "It was just a franchise that had lived in the bottom for too long," Donovan said. "Ownership clearly had lost interest and fans had lost interest. Even though there were a lot of great stories on that team, we were always up against the big picture. It never felt—from the day I got there, it never felt like, 'Oh, yeah, let's unpack and buy a house and stick around.' It never had that kind of feel to it."

Shinn took the Hornets to New Orleans, of course. But Shinn, who was worth an estimated $100 million in 2010, cut ties entirely with the Sting, making them property of the league. "They took the franchise and left," Reeve said. "You can't make this stuff up. There were moving trucks at the training facility taking the stuff and leaving. It was kind of hard to watch, kind of hard to go through. I started to wonder: *Is this really where I want to be? The WNBA—is this the kind of stuff that it's going to be like?*"

It was, indeed, what it was going to be like. Reeve found a job with Dan Hughes on the Cleveland Rockers' staff in 2003. That team made the playoffs, lost to the Detroit Shock, and then folded at the end of 2003, the Cleveland Cavaliers having decided to cut ties with them after the Rockers averaged 7,399 fans per game. "I have invested in [the Rockers] now for seven years trying to find a business model for it to work in our marketplace," then–Cavs owner Gordon Gund told the Associated Press. "The fans we had were very enthusiastic. We just didn't have enough of them."

Thirteen members of the 2002–03 Cleveland Cavaliers—Zydrunas Ilgauskas, Tyrone Hill, Nick Anderson, Ricky Davis, Michael Stewart, Darius Miles, Bimbo Coles, Dajuan Wagner, Chris Mihm, DeSagana Diop, Jumaine Jones, J. R. Reid, and Milt Palacio—each made more money that season than the entire Cleveland Rockers' roster combined, which was capped at $622,000 per the WNBA's collective bargaining agreement. Of those 13 listed, 11 of them made at least twice as much as the entire Rockers' roster. Ilgauskas's $12,375,000 salary was just less than *20 times* as much as what the entire Rockers team made. For that outlay, Gund's Cavs finished 17–65, and their attendance of 11,496 fans per game ranked dead last among NBA teams. They did, however, finish third in the NBA in pace, so they did all this losing of money and games quickly. And no, the Cleveland Cavaliers did not fold after the 2002–03 season.

So Reeve returned to the Sting, who were being run by Robert L. Johnson as a condition of his getting the expansion Charlotte Bobcats in the NBA. The investment and enthusiasm that engendered was predictable, while the Sting's attempted rebuild led to trading Dawn Staley and a dip in interest as well. Lacey had taken over when Donovan bolted west to the Seattle Storm. (Donovan won a title there with Sue Bird as her point guard in 2004, defeating the Connecticut Sun and rookie point guard Lindsay Whalen.) Lacey's top assistant on that team? Cheryl Reeve.

By late in the 2005 season, the Bobcats had a problem. Muggsy Bogues, the 5'3" Hornets star and household name in Charlotte, wanted to be the Bobcats' television analyst. The Bobcats, run by Ed Tapscott (who also ran the Sting in his spare time, and once, while running the New York Knicks, drafted Frederic Weis) didn't want that. Here's how the *Charlotte Observer* reported what happened next: "So Tapscott invited Bogues to a Sting game recently. At half-time, Tapscott asked Bogues if he would be interested in coaching the Sting."

The hiring was part of a hot new trend the WNBA had discovered, a talent pool that hadn't previously been tapped: men. Back in its inaugural season, seven of eight WNBA teams were coached by women. Bogues made the Sting the ninth of 13 teams to be coached by men in 2005. This despite the fact that 19 of 26 assistants at the time were women, including Lin Dunn and Marianne Stanley. But the 2003 WNBA Finals, coached by Bill Laimbeer of the Detroit Shock and Michael Cooper of the Los Angeles Sparks, convinced many men that the solution to a team's coaching opening had to be a man, preferably one with NBA playing experience. As usual, isolated success for men was applied broadly in sports, just as sustained success by women is so often written off as unrepeatable glory.

When asked about the trend a few weeks earlier, Reeve expressed optimism that the change was merely temporary. "It's disappointing but not discouraging," Reeve said in July 2004. "There will be a time. I know as I pay my dues, I gain knowledge—not only from Trudi but from scouting Laimbeer and Cooper. I feel like I'm going to be well equipped when my [name] is called."

Reeve chose not to return and coach as an assistant under Bogues, who had no previous coaching experience whatsoever and led the Sting to an 11–23 mark in 2006 before Johnson, now in control of the Bobcats, folded the Sting. (Incidentally, the Bobcats—later renamed the Hornets—finished no higher than 22nd in the NBA in attendance during Johnson's tenure as owner, and they just twice (barely) cracked the top 20 in NBA team attendance during Michael Jordan's decade-plus at the helm. At no point did anyone seriously suggest folding the Hornets.)

The Detroit Shock had also been vulnerable, but Laimbeer personally lobbied the Pistons' owners to keep the team, which began the 2002 season 0–10, running into 2003. That proved to be an important thing, not only for the Shock but for women's basketball's most important collaboration.

After Knox completed her master's in education, she was offered a chance to teach undergraduate classes while pursuing a second master's, this time a double master's in women's sports and sociology. While there, she also began doing sales and marketing work for the Ladies Professional Golf Association (LPGA), giving her critical business-side experience to go with her educational bona fides. Knox loved academia, but she was ready to get into the arena. "That's what I'm so passionate about, fighting the fight for all marginalized groups, and that sport can really show people the way, if you will," Knox said. "That's really what makes me tick and why I am so passionate about what I've lived through, and I don't want anybody else to go through that."

That fall, Knox had two job offers: one from U.S. Soccer, and one from the Detroit Shock as director of sales and marketing. "I grew up on the Bad Boys, loved Bill Laimbeer, and [Joe] Dumars, the Microwave [Vinnie Johnson], and Isiah Thomas back in the day,"

Knox said. "All growing up, ironically enough, I wore No. 11 because I loved Isiah Thomas. I was a point guard [in basketball]. At the time the Pistons' president convinced me that I'd be doing more good fighting the fight for women's athletics by coming to work for them."

The Shock had also done some unwitting recruiting of Knox the year before, when Carley and her father sat among 22,076 fans, a WNBA record, and watched Laimbeer's Shock deny Lisa Leslie and the Sparks a third straight WNBA title, avenging Cheryl's 2001 Sting in the process.

Knox said:

I'll never forget sitting and watching that 2003 WNBA Championship Game where the Detroit Shock won and I was sitting with my father and we were losing our minds. It was one of the biggest crowds ever in the history of the WNBA, and seeing all those people there cheering and screaming and losing their minds for the Detroit Shock to go from worst to first. It was an incredibly moving experience, and similar to watching the women's national team win the gold medal in Atlanta and being in that stadium in Georgia, and all those people were there cheering women's athletics.

It was like they were a part of something so much bigger than themselves. It was like, "Oh my God, we're making an impact on history here." Those moments and the moments that we've had in those Game 5s where I come into the arena and am looking at a sold-out arena—those are emotional experiences. It's like, "Oh my God. All these people get it. They get it and they're here and we're together and we're doing something so much bigger." I look around the arena and I get tears in my eyes.

So Carley took the job with the Shock. Knox had been there for a year when Reeve took an interview she thought, as she entered it, would be a waste of time—lead assistant to Bill Laimbeer and the Detroit Shock for the 2006 season.

In fact, Reeve was leaning toward not coaching at all in 2006. She'd been burned in Charlotte, then Cleveland, then Charlotte again. Her father had been diagnosed with cancer—multiple myeloma. And then Bill Laimbeer called her.

Reeve recalled, laughing:

> And I hated Bill. I was like, "No way. I'm not going to go work for this guy." Because when I was in Cleveland, especially, I worked for Dan, and Bill just brings out the best/worst in you if you're competitive. He's smart, he's competitive, and he brings it out in you. I didn't think I could ever go work for this guy.
>
> I can still see walking into this conference room, and Rick [Mahorn] was in there, and Bill was in there, and the two of them, the way that they bantered back and forth, they were a lot of fun because they were former teammates. Rick was just a fun guy. I felt instantly comfortable and being able to be myself.
>
> The types of questions, or maybe the conversation we had, were very real. Bill is so direct. And it's just something I found that I really enjoyed. . . . I could just say what I wanted to say. And that became apparent very, very quickly. And I think it was ultimately Bill's appeal to me to be the person that would come in and give the team the direction they needed in terms of attention to detail.
>
> It was in my wheelhouse. It was what I felt like I was good at. He was saying, "Look. We won a championship in

'03. We got to the playoffs in '04 and '05. The team is telling me we need this. We think you happen to be somebody that could help us potentially."

And so it was one of those things. It was absolutely the right button.

The traditionalist in Reeve felt like she needed to be home, but Laimbeer was incredibly supportive, she said, telling her anytime she needed to go back to Jersey to be there for a test or an important milestone: "Go, go do it."

But mostly what Cheryl Reeve did in Detroit was to go break down film, find the weaknesses in the Shock's opponents, and then communicate them to a young, balanced team filled with players in their mid-20s such as Swin Cash, Deanna Nolan, and Cheryl Ford, and led by the legendary Katie Smith, then 32 and absolutely still in her prime.

By late July it was understood that the Shock, after a 16–18 2005, were once again title contenders. And as the *Detroit Free Press* reckoned with the reasons, one of them was clearly Cheryl Reeve:

> Armed with state-of-the-art video technology, she scouts opponents for several hours a day, looking for any tendencies that could give the Shock the edge.
>
> Her contributions were a direct reason why the Shock limited Lisa Leslie, the greatest center in WNBA history, to 10 points in Friday's 73–59 win over the league-best Sparks.
>
> "I really enjoy looking for things that will, basically, frustrate the heck out of them at game time," Reeve said. "We take pride in the fact that when people play us, they don't get what they like."

Cheryl was in many ways the same non-partier she had been in high school, and at La Salle—preferring to bury herself in work over seeking out new people. A standard night her first year on Laimbeer's staff was grabbing spinach dip and apple walnut salad at Applebee's, settling in for hours of breaking down film, and discovering precisely what the Shock players needed to know about defending their next opponent—to give them no choice but to at least *know* what they needed to do. Laimbeer was in charge of motivating them to do it.

But Cheryl also found herself falling into a new group, thanks to her role conducting league business for the Shock. The Shock offices were located at the Palace of Auburn Hills, but the fax machine was reserved for business operations one floor up. So anytime the Shock wanted to sign or release a player, they needed to send the paperwork in by trudging up to the business office. That's where Reeve met Knox, in the midst of a WNBA transaction.

Carley recognized Cheryl was new in town and started including her in everything her group of friends did. But was it love at first sight? Not according to Cheryl:

> No. No. I thought, *There's no way*. We drove each other nuts. Yeah, no, it was definitely not instant. I think she would say the same thing.
>
> It was more of a friendship of—I didn't have anybody else and she was established there, had a big group of friends. She's the exact opposite of myself. She likes a lot of people and she's the reason why I even have any friends, because I'm just not very good at that. I would always say I would be very much fine alone. I guess that's . . . When I say *alone*, I don't mean . . . Like, I like people.

An all-female American team plays basketball in 1899. *FPG/Getty Images*

Peps Neuman poses for a player portrait with the Arkansas Gems in 1983. *Star Tribune via Getty Images*

Peps Neuman fires up the University of Minnesota crowd at a 2014 game.
Neuman continues this tradition at Minnesota home games to this day.
Jerry Holt/Star Tribune via Getty Images

Minnesota Lynx president of business operations Carley Knox (shown here in 1998) was a fierce soccer player who went on to star at Ohio University.

Coaches Cheryl Reeve (back row, left) and Carley Knox (back row, right) pose with their Kenwood Park team.

Legendary Minnesota Golden Gophers guard Lindsay Whalen, who went on to star in the WNBA, including with the Minnesota Lynx, directs the Golden Gophers during her tenure as University of Minnesota head coach. *Star Tribune/AP*

Minnesota Lynx players Maya Moore and Seimone Augustus rally their teammates during the 2016 WNBA semifinals. *AP*

Minnesota head coach Cheryl Reeve says goodbye to veteran center Sylvia Fowles after the player's final game.

Rachel Banham was a Minnesota
Lynx fan from an early age. *Courtesy
of Rachel Banham*

Banham starred at the University of Minnesota, and eventually returned home to play
for the Lynx.

Minnesota standout Mara Braun fights for a bucket against Michigan in 2023. *AP*

Paige Bueckers, shown here in 2022 with the UConn Huskies, returned home to play in the 2022 Final Four right in Minneapolis. *SPTSW/AP*

But I'm just not great at—I don't stay in touch. I have
friends that, thank goodness, they have the persistence to
stay in touch. So I was just never really good [at it]. I was
just like my dad when it came to that. And my mom. I don't
think they were ever really that social. . . . So I think I kind
of picked that up.

But for Carley, the passion she poured into her work with the
Shock was the same with which she approached everything. Carley
didn't just play a little music in high school and college; she played
in several bands and recorded a CD. Same thing when she got out
to Minneapolis: a second band, this one all women, and another CD.
There were no half-measures with Carley Knox, and that extended to
her social life, too. Knox recalled:

> I've always been a social butterfly. It's the way I am per-
> sonally but it's also . . . The women's studies, the feminist
> quote, "Personal is politics, politics are personal." To me
> it was living and breathing the WNBA every single day
> as well. I love being around people, I love those relation-
> ships, but also it's living and breathing, and that's what
> you're doing every single day with the Detroit Shock in the
> WNBA and grass roots and growing these things through
> my personal relationships. Whether people truly were
> WNBA fans or whether they were coming out to support
> Cheryl and I personally, that's the way you have to get it
> done in women's athletics. People need to feel so person-
> ally connected not just to the product but to the people
> behind their product as well.

What Knox was doing on the business side was working. The Shock finished third in the WNBA in attendance in 2005, then surged to first in 2006, where they remained for the next three years. And Cheryl's video breakdowns, the talented roster, and the motivation of Laimbeer all led to the kind of success both Cheryl and Bill left their meeting believing was possible for the Shock.

Knox watched 19,671 people fill Joe Louis Arena for Game 5 of the 2006 WNBA Finals, tangible proof of her ability to make substantive change in the world of women's sports. (That the Shock had to give up their primary home court to a Mariah Carey concert for Game 5 of the WNBA Finals is almost unfathomable, but Knox and the Shock filled the second arena anyway.)

And then, in a game decided by the slimmest of margins, the Shock won the 2006 WNBA title 80–75 over Nicole Powell, Rebekkah Brunson, and the Sacramento Monarchs. Deanna Nolan scored 24 and was named Finals MVP. Katie Smith scored 17 and added 6 assists. The postgame locker room was pandemonium, champagne and Colt 45 in equal amounts being liberally poured and consumed. A city that had experienced plenty of heartbreak, and had nearly lost its saving grace of a team, embraced the once-endangered franchise.

As Michael Rosenberg wrote that night in the *Detroit Free Press*: "Yeah, these are the glory days for Detroit sports franchises, unless you happen to care about the playoffs. Then not so much. But while the Pistons and Wings fell short and the Tigers' fate is TBD, at least one Detroit team came through." History would not be kind to the 2006 Tigers, either.

The run of success continued for the Detroit Shock. In 2007 they finished the regular season a league-best 24–10, beat Tamika

Catchings and the Indiana Fever (Nolan had 30) to reach the WNBA Finals, where they faced the Phoenix Mercury. They took a 2–1 lead in that best-of-five series against the Mercury before losing Game 4, and then the incredible trinity of Diana Taurasi, Cappie Pondexter, and Penny Taylor combined for 73 in a Game 5 win. The Shock finished one win away from a third title in five years, despite a season-long conflict between Laimbeer and Swin Cash, both discussing it openly following the Game 5 loss, and ultimately leading to Cash joining Seattle in 2008.

The Shock, undaunted, came right back in 2008 and won another WNBA title, Smith and Nolan supplemented by another great season off the bench from Plenette Pierson. Once again, the Detroit Shock led the WNBA in attendance. Carley and Cheryl were thriving. Knox was being groomed to take over as COO of the WNBA team. Reeve, like many Laimbeer assistants, was being trained by Laimbeer for a head coaching gig—mentoring that Laimbeer took very seriously and would later do with Katie Smith in New York. With an eye toward that, Reeve was given a dual role, also serving as director of player personnel.

After a lopsided Detroit win over Washington that ultimately cost Mystics head coach Tree Rollins his job, Reeve told the *Courier-Post*:

> After eight years, it's kind of the plan, the progression. The way they generally do it in our league is that the head coach title goes along with being the GM. It was a big step to enhance my marketability.
>
> My growth in Detroit has been gradual. I've always done the same thing—prepare for the draft and scout—but making

trades and acquisitions has been a little more involved than at previous stops.

It's always been the goal since entering the league. I think I'm a quality assistant, but I've always aspired to have my own gig. I've got the ego it takes and want to do my own thing.

And even as the Shock closed in on another title, Laimbeer began to wonder if he was getting in the way of progress, for both Reeve and Mahorn. Between Games 2 and 3 of the 2008 WNBA Finals, Laimbeer said:

> I feel like I'm getting in the way of my two assistants. It's becoming their time, and it bothers me. But at the same time, I'm enjoying what I'm doing. At some point, I'll move on. I don't necessarily think it's right now. But I don't know.
>
> I'll go down to Florida, launch a boat. I want to get in the woods and sit in the tree stand and look for some deer, and then figure out what I want to do.

Heading into 2009 there was every reason to believe the future for the Shock, and for Reeve and Knox within the organization, was remarkably bright. The two knew their futures were connected as well—"We were a package deal by then," Reeve said—and every indication was that they'd build that future in the Motor City.

If 2008 had been a year of change—the election of Barack Obama to the presidency, a historic economic collapse, and the ushering in of a new era, all containing progressive change across race, gender, and sexuality lines in this country, the speed of and backlash to which are continuing to play out to this day—the seeds of change within the world of the Detroit Shock were fully visible only in retrospect to many of those involved.

There were Laimbeer's comments about getting out of the way of his assistants. The longtime owner of the Pistons and original owner of the Shock, Bill Davidson, would die in 2009, and there was Katie Smith, at the celebration the night the Shock won the 2008 title, getting on the microphone to express the hope that "Mrs. D keeps this thing going." Imagine that: The greatest scorer, perhaps the greatest player of her generation, on the night she led her team to another championship—"This was Katie Smith's series," Laimbeer correctly said that night—forced to make a public plea for the team she played on to exist. A team then–WNBA president Donna Orender said, correctly, "is a dynasty at this point—fourth trip to the Finals in six years. It does make them one of the most successful pro sports franchises in any league in this decade."

It could have been Detroit, the model Cheryl and Carley eventually built in Minnesota. It probably should have been Detroit. Not instead but in addition to. "Absolutely no doubt," Knox said of whether Detroit could support a WNBA team. "It's just about having the right people who believe in it and are supporting it in the right way. I could absolutely go back to Detroit and have a *W* team that would work there."

The 2009 season was challenging in virtually every way. Laimbeer, three games into the season, decided it was time to quit. He pursued an NBA opening, quickly landing a job with the Minnesota Timberwolves, a move that would prove fateful for the WNBA as well. Mahorn took over as head coach, and Reeve as general manager. "It's the same ideology," Mahorn said at a press conference announcing the changes on June 18, 2009. "I may tweak a few things to put a stamp on it. Other than that, it's status quo."

It is noticeable, of course, that Mahorn got hired as the head coach, not Reeve. The dual role of GM and head coach, custom at the time, got split up, even as Mahorn reiterated at this press conference that his goal was to coach an NBA team, not a WNBA team. This is not to say he was a figure of convenience in the WNBA the way some other NBA figures were at that time. But it reflects the promotion of someone who unapologetically cast the WNBA as a steppingstone over Reeve, a women's basketball lifer.

Even Mahorn cast the division of labor in a way that elevated Reeve. "The maturity will help, and the tutelage from Bill and Cheryl," Mahorn said, sitting next to Reeve at the press conference. "I've learned what to do from my coaching experience, and I'll get the chance to apply it now."

And for her part, Katie Smith saw the group as a unit, and expected more of the same: "They were all in it together. You take one of them away, and it's still functioning. They've been learning from each other, so it's not a shocker to me that Ricky's taking over. It doesn't change a whole lot—the philosophy, the style. It'll be little tweaks here and there, but it'll be the same M.O. It'll be getting used to a new vibe."

Reeve recalled her time with Mahorn fondly years later as well. Cheryl told me in 2018:

> "[We were] kind of a unique duo. Rick and I had a strong relationship. We were good together. It was more of a partnership in the way we approached it. It was tremendous in terms of how you had to think. I felt like I thought more

like a head coach even though I was still in an assistant coach role. Rick allowed me to take on [anything, even] the offense. . . . He didn't have an ego about it. He wasn't like, 'Hey, no. This is my gig. Stay seated.' He was collaborative, which is what I appreciated about him."

Laimbeer didn't leave on anything approaching bad terms. He praised his assistants again, as he had always been quick to do during his WNBA career: "[Rick]'s more than capable, and with Cheryl they did a lot of the work anyway. . . . Cheryl and Rick had a lot of say about personnel and decisions we made on the floor."

Laimbeer joined the team just over a month later at the White House, where President Barack Obama welcomed them (after expressing his surprise, as a lifelong Bulls fan, that he was congratulating iconic Pistons Laimbeer and Mahorn), receiving a Shock jersey from Cheryl Ford and Katie Smith and giving a speech about what the Shock and the WNBA meant writ large. His theme? Permanence. He said:

> Let me also say something as a father—I was mentioning it to the team before we came out. It's hard to believe the WNBA has already been around for twelve years. And that means that my daughters have never known a time when women couldn't play professional sports.
>
> They look at the TV and they see me watching *Sports-Center* and they see young women who look like them on the screen. And that lets them and all our young women, as well as young men, know that we should take for granted that women are going to thrive and excel as athletes. And it makes my daughters look at themselves differently, to see that they can be champions too.

So as a father, I want to say thank you. And thank you
to all the WNBA athletes who work hard each day to set
a positive example to which all our daughters can aspire.

Injuries took their toll on the 2009 Shock, who fell to 9–14 with
a 79–75 loss at home to old friend Swin Cash and the Seattle Storm,
despite 29 points from Deanna Nolan. "The first half, I didn't know
if that was the Shock team or somebody else's team," Mahorn said
after the game. "The second half, we came back and shut them down,
but unfortunately, we couldn't get the win. If I could have had seven
or eight timeouts, I would have probably called them all in the first
half to see if we were going to show up."

He said it to an Associated Press reporter, but the story didn't
appear in the *Detroit Free Press*, nor was there a beat reporter or a
columnist there from the newspaper. The biggest draw in the WNBA
in 2008, with a sold-out championship just months before, did not
rate regular coverage from the city's newspaper in 2009—not one
bylined story in August, for instance.

By September the Shock managed to climb back into the playoff
race. Deanna Nolan earned WNBA Player of the Week honors. And
yet the team quickly fell back into old habits of promotion. A rare
item on the Shock in the *Free Press* advertised a free ticket offer for
Friday night, September 4, against Tamika Catchings and Indiana.
"This year, a lot of people will be around for the holiday weekend,"
Shock COO Craig Turnbull said. "This is a great chance for people
that haven't made it out to the Palace for a game yet this season."

That day, the *Free Press* reported Laimbeer officially signing on
with the Minnesota Timberwolves as an assistant coach. It did not

have a game story, not even a box score, from Detroit's win over Indiana.

The next mention of the Shock? An offer of free tickets in exchange for giving blood at the Palace at Auburn Hills on September 7, the day after Nolan's 19 points at that same venue earned the Shock their third straight win, 84–75 over the Chicago Sky, and pushed Detroit above .500 to 16–15.

Knox said:

> It was a wonderful thing that we owned our building and had all these concert venues and, obviously, had an NBA team. At one point there was an arena football team. At one point there was a hockey team. We had a lot going on there. It was a wonderful thing to have so many wonderful assets at our fingertips to leverage and sell.
>
> But at the same time, their business model was, they did a lot of the vouchering to make money on concessions, merch, parking, etc. . . . And if you're giving free tickets out in the market at a gas station, for example, you are incredibly devaluing your product and how people will view and value your own products. If you don't evaluate yourself to make sure that people are actually paying and valuing the product, how could you expect the community to value it?

Even the semifinal series against the Indiana Fever did not merit game coverage, the series curtain-raiser a mere sidebar in length. The final game in Detroit for the Shock, a 72–56 win over Indiana in front of 7,214 fans, was not mentioned in the next day's *Free Press*.

As she so often did, Tamika Catchings elevated her game and that of her team to another level, and the Fever won the next two games to reach the WNBA Finals. Detroit had eliminated Indiana from the playoffs the previous three seasons. "Finally!" Catchings exclaimed at the postgame presser. "I've been waiting for this for eight years." She went on to discuss how any trip to the WNBA Finals in the Eastern Conference would always have to go through Detroit.

And reinforcements were set to return to the roster. Katie Smith missed the final 12 games with a bulging disc in her back. Plenette Pierson missed the entire season after shoulder surgery, and Cheryl Ford missed time with a knee injury. Shavonte Zellous made the all-rookie team after the Shock selected her eleventh overall in the 2009 draft. Only DeWanna Bonner, Angel McCoughtry, and Kristi Toliver managed to accumulate more win shares out of that 2009 WNBA rookie crop. Perry A. Farrell wrote in the *Free Press* on September 28, 2009, that "the Shock should be one of the favorites," though he began that sentence with the caveat, "If there is a WNBA next season."

And Mahorn sounded upbeat about the team's future as well. "I haven't heard anything about the league folding," Mahorn said. "I've heard that Atlanta might be moving, but other than that, if we're here, I'll be here . . . we'll get ready for what's going to happen in the draft and free agency and see what will make our team even better."

As for the business side, yes, the Shock saw a drop in average attendance, ending its run atop the WNBA. But in the epicenter of the worst economic collapse since the Great Depression, in the city hit hardest by it, the Shock still ranked fifth in the WNBA at 8,000 fans per game.

But it was the most challenging year yet for Cheryl and Carley. They'd earned a much-needed vacation, and packed their bags for a rest and recharge in Provincetown, Massachusetts. They'd checked their bags and were waiting by the gate when someone—they don't remember who, but it was a family member, Cheryl believes—called to ask a confusing question: "Why, when we try to go to the Detroit Shock website, is it redirecting us to a Tulsa Shock site?"

Carley and Cheryl quickly started calling around to Shock front-office people before ultimately learning the truth: Without telling the staff, Mrs. D had sold the Detroit Shock to an ownership group fronted by Bill Cameron, an Oklahoma City businessman who had been actively and publicly seeking a WNBA franchise. Part of the ownership group was also Nolan Richardson, a successful men's coach at the University of Arkansas with a national title on his résumé, and Cameron had announced that any team he came to own would install Richardson as head coach and general manager. Richardson had never coached women's basketball at any level, or even men's pro basketball.

Cheryl and Carley never got on that plane. "So we were sitting at the gate," Cheryl remembered. "Our bags were checked. We walked and went back to the gate-check area down where ticketing was and said, 'We're not getting on the flight. We need our bags.' So we waited for our bags and grabbed our bags. And we went back home because we knew it was about to hit. And Carley wanted to be there for her staff."

Pistons president Tom Wilson gathered the entire Shock front office and explained that the decision had been made to cease operations in Detroit. The reason Wilson said he had been given by the Davidson family—which infuriated Reeve—was that the team, over a period of several years, had lost $20 million. The Detroit Pistons, meanwhile, were paying well in excess of $20 million to several men not to coach their team—Larry Brown alone had been bought out two years into his five-year, $25 million contract. "And I thought, *How dare we lose $20 million the way that we lost $20 million, as opposed to that they throw around $20 million,*" Reeve said. "I am infuriated by it all, and bitter. Carley's a way better person when it comes to stuff like this. She was able to have perspective and say, 'It's important here that we end the right way.' And I was like, 'Well, you get to do that. I don't have to do that. I'm pissed and I'm never going to talk to these people again.' That's more my way." She declined a chance to serve as Nolan Richardson's assistant.

That proved wise. The way things ended in Detroit soured so many vital members of the franchise on continuing to Tulsa. Katie Smith went to Washington. Deanna Nolan—pride of Flint, Michigan—simply never played in the WNBA again, preferring to stay overseas, even after the New York Liberty and their general manager, Bill Laimbeer, acquired her rights in 2013.

Nolan told Michigan Live in 2015:

> I decided to leave. I didn't return to the Shock because of the relocation, and I didn't want to start over. I've played with the Shock my entire career and thought it would end there. I didn't want to play nowhere else.
>
> My favorite memories were winning the three championships, so I was very disappointed in the way things ended in Detroit. There were never any talks of the team possibly moving, and I found out when I was overseas.

By the middle of Richardson's first season in Tulsa in 2010, none of the Detroit Shock from the previous season were still on the roster.

The Shock finished 6–28, and despite building around Marion Jones (who hadn't played competitive basketball in 13 years) and lottery pick Liz Cambage, and convincing 40-year-old Sheryl Swoopes to come out of retirement, the Shock began 1–10 in 2011 before Richardson resigned, never to coach in the WNBA again.

The question of where this left Knox and Reeve professionally was a more complicated one. Knox said:

> Obviously it was a really, really challenging time. I'm think-ing back to the amount of time we spent in our townhouse just talking through what we were going to do and [if we] were . . . going to different cities. I had some pretty incred-ible job offers across the WNBA and, as I mentioned, was being groomed for COO [in Detroit]. It was an incredibly challenging time trying to figure out what was the next step for me. I didn't want to burn any bridges. I thought that was really important despite the pain of, *How could this possibly happen? We've won three championships [and had] some of the biggest crowds ever in the WNBA.* Not a perfect business model by any means, but we had started to build something pretty incredible here in Detroit, and wrapping our heads [around] it wasn't easy.

Reeve had interviewed for two previous head coaching posi-tions—at one she simply didn't see a pathway to contention fast enough, and at the other, her philosophy differed from the owner on how to build a team. She was eager to get her shot but also understood that it needed to be the right gig. Every mentor she'd had, from Joe McKeown to Bill Laimbeer, had emphasized that to her.

Reeve and the players at least had the option to stay or go. Knox was determined to end things the right way—in part to preserve her future professional prospects and in part because she had tremendous respect for Tom Wilson—and so it fell to her to have to fire every member of her staff. Bill Cameron and his partner David Box wanted their own people on the business side in Tulsa. "Laying off our staff was one of the hardest things I've ever been through in my life," Knox said. "We were there for two of the three championships and are really one of the greatest WNBA teams ever. It was really, really trying and awful to break up that staff and what we had built there."

Next, Carley was assigned a task that was almost unfathomably cruel. She was asked to call every single Detroit Shock season ticket holder and ask if that person would like to become a Detroit Pistons single ticket holder, to provide financial support to the organization that had just killed the Detroit Shock. "I think it was an uphill battle for me," Carley said with a small laugh. "Let's just say that. There were a lot of really, really upset people who were yelling at me, when obviously I had nothing to do with that decision. It was more nursing them through those hard times, and eventually some of those people did become Detroit Pistons fans and did go back."

Her ability to sell even Pistons tickets to Shock fans impressed Tom Wilson so much, he offered her a chance to stay and work on the NBA side of the building. "I'll never forget sitting in his office and having this conversation when I respectfully declined the position that they had offered me to stay on and work on the men's side with them," Knox said. "It was an incredible compliment. To this day he's still a reference to me on my résumé. I'm so glad that

I didn't just lay my staff off and then move along despite it being completely brutal."

But while the emotional toll of the Detroit Shock destruction still haunts Knox and Reeve to this day, it did provide clarity to each of them for what they were looking for in their next professional gig. Knox understood that wherever she ended up—and she had job offers from WNBA teams across the league—it needed to be for an owner who was truly invested in the women's game. "Ultimately, not just in Detroit but with any professional sports team, it's about what you put into it and how your own leadership values it," Knox said. "What resources are you putting behind it? What kind of staff are you putting behind it? Are you treating it like the stepchild or are you truly believing in the product and saying, 'This is absolutely something that can be profitable for us and can be a wonderful venture. Oh, by the way, it would be a wonderful thing for society and our community in showing the world what's possible.'"

And Reeve made a decision for herself that she not only wasn't going to be Nolan Richardson's assistant. She wasn't going to be anybody's assistant. She said:

> I can still see sitting at my desk in Detroit in our office and having this mindset, "Look, I've been here before. This is the third team!" I made a decision long ago that in the WNBA there would be some harder things, some harder times, but staying the course was really important in those times. Prepare yourself financially . . .
>
> And I thought, *I'm not going to Tulsa to be Nolan Richardson's assistant coach.* Because that was sort of the offer. No freaking way. I said, "I'm tired of this shit. I'm 10 years

in. I'm more than qualified to have my own gig." And I
thought, *I'm going to reach out to a few people that I value
and just say, "Hey, I'm no longer going to be an assistant
coach in the WNBA. I'm going to be a head coach. Let me
know if you ever have interest."*

One of those places was Minnesota. And fortune would smile on
the Lynx, Reeve, and Knox alike. Jennifer Gillom had served as interim
head coach during the 2009 season, but when contract talks stalled,
the Los Angeles Sparks swooped in and snatched Gillom away. That
left the Lynx in need of a head coach just as executive Roger Griffith
received Reeve's email.

To this day, Roger Griffith insists that Bill Laimbeer had nothing
to do with hiring Reeve. Laimbeer is equally insistent that he receive
the credit for it. "And I believe it," Reeve said, referring to Laimbeer's
version of events, "Because . . . he can be very persistent. Roger said
it had nothing to do with Bill, but I think it probably did on some
level. I think Bill had to give him the confidence to be able to go to
him and say, 'What about Cheryl's situation? What have you seen?'
Versus if Bill wasn't here."

And while Reeve and Knox were, in fact, a package deal, the Lynx
didn't have an executive position comparable to the director of sales
and marketing spot Knox had occupied in Detroit, despite the fact
that the Lynx were coming off a season finishing just ninth in the
WNBA in attendance, well behind Detroit. Reeve said:

> Carley's career is important to her, important to me. Car-
> ley was the top salesperson in the league. This organization
> didn't necessarily pounce on that opportunity. I don't know

what the thought process was when the team—standard practice would be in sports that if something happens, and there's a coach or a player that you could scoop up, that you might go, "Hey." I feel bad for her, but that didn't necessarily happen.

But it worked out through my agent at the time. Expressed what was important. And then, so Carley actually went backward in her role, which I said to Carley, "It kind of sucks, but it's the situation we're in."

Carley put it more simply: "I definitely took a step back in my career for the position that I came here for, but you do crazy things for love, right?"

It was a whirlwind for both of them. On October 19, 2009, they found out the Detroit Shock no longer existed. By December 8, Reeve was hired as head coach of the Minnesota Lynx. By January 10, both Knox and Reeve were employees of the Minnesota Lynx and had moved to Minneapolis.

Reeve could have been forgiven for focusing on simply opening boxes for a few days. But she'd already been to Connecticut in late December to scout Tina Charles, then a senior and the consensus top prospect in the upcoming WNBA Draft. And by January 2010, she was ready for her first order of business with the Minnesota Lynx: trading for Lindsay Whalen. (Okay, it was technically her second order of business, as the Lynx had taken Rebekkah Brunson in the dispersal draft a week after Reeve was hired, but that was a no-brainer.)

CHAPTER 7

"THIS IS WHAT WE DO!"

———

TO UNDERSTAND MINNESOTA basketball in the latter half of the first decade of the 2000s is to know it by an absence, specifically that of Lindsay Whalen. The Gophers honored her by retiring her number in January 2005, and had some success after, reaching the Sweet 16 that season and making another three NCAA tournaments before the end of the decade. But the gap between Minnesota and the elite teams in both the Big Ten and the country as a whole seemed only to grow larger, while the Lynx floundered despite the presence of the great Seimone Augustus, and the state cried out for Whalen as a savior.

In January 2007 the Lynx passed up a chance to add Janel McCarville, Whalen's interior counterpart on the Final Four Gophers, and writer Pamela Schmid, in the lede of a *Star Tribune* piece, compared the decision to the Lynx passing up the chance to draft Whalen. Three weeks later, Gophers senior captain Kelly Roysland broke her collarbone, and both *Star Tribune* Gophers writer Jerry Zgoda and Gophers head coach Pam Borton compared the moment to when Whalen broke her hand as a senior and found a way to play through it.

The Minnesota Gophers didn't make the tournament that season, but New Mexico, featuring Minnesota native Amy Beggin, reached the Big Dance, and the *Star Tribune* offered this scouting report about her: "The freshman looks a little like her favorite player, Lindsay Whalen. Plays a wee bit like her too."

And that was all in a two-month span in 2007.

"I remember when the Gophers—when Lindsay and Janel were just top dogs and just really, really good," Rachel Banham—who has come the closest to actually playing like Whalen since Whalen herself—told me in a 2022 interview when I asked what her earliest basketball memory was. "That's just a vivid memory of mine. It's just when they turned the program around and got buckets and got to the Final Four."

The primary problem with bringing Lindsay Whalen back to Minnesota, to play with the Lynx, was that she was under contract with the Connecticut Sun, and they had a full understanding of just how lucky they were to employ Lindsay Whalen. Sun coach Mike Thibault was not a sentimental man when it came to winning basketball games. And from the moment he had selected Whalen in the 2004 WNBA Draft, he'd handed her the ball and let her run his team in Connecticut—into the WNBA Finals in the first two seasons and the playoffs every season thereafter through 2008.

Still, Lynx general manager Roger Griffith would check in on Whalen with his Sun counterpart, Chris Sienko, from time to time. "It's two teams wanting the same thing," Griffith told Lyndsey D'Arcangelo of the *Athletic* in 2019. "I would say they were more conversations like, 'Has anything changed for anybody?' Not anything in-depth, not anything serious. Connecticut was doing well at the time. They got to a couple Finals, and they weren't really motivated to want to trade. They had a good team going."

But in 2009 the Sun finally fell short of the postseason and ended up with the second overall pick in the 2010 draft. The Lynx held the top pick, and Tina Charles, who everyone recognized would be the next great star in the WNBA, was finishing her senior season, which would end with her Connecticut Huskies 39–0, unstoppable between Charles and a junior guard named Maya Moore.

The parameters of the deal had been agreed upon before Reeve arrived, but Griffith ran the deal by Reeve while she was moving, and she was all for it. She knew the strengths of Whalen well from breaking down video of her over the previous six years. "The main game plan was to figure out how to control her ability to get others involved and keep her out of the paint. She was such a good finisher," Reeve said. "You couldn't just play one scheme for the entire game because she was going to pick you apart. From afar, you could see the kind of competitor she was."

But Reeve also saw some habits Whalen had fallen into. She understood the Lynx needed the best possible Whalen, and the two of them met, once Whalen arrived back home, and spoke for two hours long before training camp even began. They charted a course together, and both of them left the conversation feeling like it would give them a chance to reach the success they both sought. "She gave me some really good structure," Whalen remembered. "It wasn't necessarily what I wanted to hear, but I needed to hear it. And it gave me goals—so then I had practice goals, and my efficiency went way up."

Reeve wanted Whalen as she was—tough, getting to the rim, defending, and making plays for teammates. It wasn't about turning someone who'd hit only 26.8 percent of her threes through 2009 into a gunner from deep. It was about handing her the ball and letting her run the team.

Reeve did have higher expectations for Whalen—she wanted her in better shape. She expected her productivity to go up—points, assists, even rebounding. But to Whalen's ears, it came down to Reeve wanting her to lean into being herself.

And Reeve, on the day Whalen was introduced to the Minnesota media via conference call in January—Lindsay was playing in Prague—gave an assist of her own to the business side, where Carley had officially begun that very week. "I'd like to say to all the Minnesota fans out there that it's not just about being aware that Lindsay Whalen is coming to play for the Minnesota Lynx. It's about paying for tickets to come watch Lindsay Whalen. That's really important, and that's a challenge to the fans. Yeah, we're all excited, but come watch her play."

That weekend, Lindsay Whalen could watch the Vikings play in the NFL divisional playoffs—not because she'd returned home but because the games were on satellite TV in the Czech Republic. (The Vikings beat the Cowboys but broke Whalen's heart by losing to the Saints in the NFC Championship Game the following week.)

In that first year for Whalen and Reeve, the attraction of Whalen playing for the home team again had to carry much of the excitement, because the 2010 Lynx weren't very good on the court. Expectations were high with Whalen, Augustus, and Candice Wiggins all among the USA Basketball player pool, but Augustus missed the first third of the season after having a pair of nonmalignant tumors removed, and never really found her customary level of efficiency that season, while Wiggins tore her Achilles tendon in the eighth game, was lost for the year, and never again regained that elite level over the duration of her career.

That couldn't stop the positive feeling about women's basketball across the state, though, both with the return of Whalen and the emergence of the powerhouse Lakeville North High School, which finished as the state's only undefeated team, powered by senior Cassie Rochel and junior Rachel Banham. Rochel was headed to Wisconsin to play, but Banham, referred to by the *Star Tribune* as the best point guard the state had produced since Lindsay Whalen, had committed to the Gophers. "There's really no weakness to her game," Rochel said of Banham in March 2010. "She always finds a way to pull something out of her sleeve, something that you don't see coming. She's broken so many girls' ankles, it's amazing."

Meanwhile, Reeve set about improving the Lynx defensively, and on the boards—they were already a pretty solid offensive team, in her view, even before Whalen arrived—2nd in the league in offensive rating but 12th in defensive rating and 10th in rebounding percentage. The lack of Wiggins and peak Augustus, however, offset the gains Reeve realized on the defensive end in 2010 (eighth in the league) and rebounding (fourth in the league). They added Rebekkah Brunson, remember?

In the stands, the Lynx drew 9,985 for their 2010 home opener, a loss to the Washington Mystics and old Reeve compatriot Katie Smith, who scored 16 points. Whalen had 12 points and 7 assists in her first time in front of the home fans as a Minnesota player in six years. But the season was rough in the early going, 2–9 through the first 11 games. Fortunately, the next two games came against Richardson's Shock, both Lynx wins, and Minnesota held serve for most of the rest of the season, entering an August 12 game against the Los Angeles Sparks in position to control their own playoff destiny.

That day—August 12—served as a portal into the seasons to come for the Lynx. First, Whalen officially signed a long-term contract extension to stay in Minnesota. Then came the game itself. Charde Houston came off the bench to score 16 in the first half alone, finishing with 24, and the Lynx raced out to a 17-point lead. Los Angeles fought back and took the lead late, but Whalen's two free throws with 1.1 seconds left seemed to seal the game. They did not. On the ensuing play, the Sparks found Tina Thompson on the baseline, and she sank a 17-footer at the buzzer to give the Sparks a 78–77 victory.

Reeve recalled to KYW Newsradio years later:

> I wasn't somebody that thought, *Well, maybe we'll just be bad in 2010, and we'll get Maya Moore and everything will be fine.* You know, I wanted to be a playoff team. And we were just, you know, 1.1 seconds away from being that playoff team. It's a play I'll never forget. . . .
>
> Sometimes you have to experience failure before you can get to success. And I think it's one of the best examples in my career, that without that failure, we don't get the opportunity to be in the lottery and we don't win the lottery and get Maya Moore without that difficulty in 2010.

But whether or not that was the plan, the Lynx were bad in 2010, and then they got Maya Moore, and then everything *was* fine. But it was more complicated than that. "That last road trip . . . we didn't win all three, so we didn't make the playoffs," Whalen said, recalling the trip in 2022. "We were out of the playoffs, right? But it showed us if we played together, really honed in on the defensive end, we could be successful. Now, we didn't know we were gonna go win a championship. But [we knew] we could have success."

Reeve wasn't counting on one player to change the entire franchise. So she asked Whalen at her 2010 seasonal exit interview who she wanted to play with. It was a question she felt would aid her as the team entered the offseason and serve as a reminder to Whalen that they were in this together. "I wanted to know [the answer] from her because I thought she was smart, mature, and would be able to handle it," Reeve told the *Athletic* in 2019. "There's a certain way that we wanted to do things. We knew we had some work to do in getting the right pieces. I think she was shocked when I asked her. It's a big responsibility, and she didn't take that lightly. Some players shy away from that; they don't want to hurt anybody's feelings. Lindsay took that very seriously. So we sat there and tried to formulate a roster going forward."

It is easy, in retrospect, to look at the 2011 Minnesota Lynx on paper and think that anybody could have led them to a WNBA title. That a team featuring Lindsay Whalen, Maya Moore, Seimone Augustus, and Rebekkah Brunson would be unbeatable. But consider the egos it was necessary to navigate, the extent to which the primary stars needed to buy in to a vision from a head coach with one season and a 13–21 record at the helm.

Seimone Augustus predated everyone with the Minnesota Lynx. She'd been there since 2006. And it isn't an exaggeration to say that since childhood she'd been tabbed not only to become a superstar but to take the sport itself to another level. Augustus remembered becoming so famous, so early, saying, "I couldn't walk through a mall in Baton Rouge after I turned 11." By her freshman year of high school, she was featured on the cover of *Sports Illustrated for Women*—the first cover of that brand-new magazine—with the question: "Is she the next Michael Jordan?"

Augustus told me in 2018:

> Having the spotlight on you early obviously changes everything for you. You gotta carry yourself differently. You gotta think differently. You gotta do things differently, because you understand at that age that you're not just representing yourself. People are watching you. I think that's the thing. People are watching you to see you either do well or make a mistake or whatever. But eyes are on you, and so you can't have the luxury of being an 11-year-old and playing and having friends and doing all this stuff—the carefree thoughts 11-year-olds have.
>
> It definitely helped build character early in me and helped me understand the whole perception of what people think and see and believe about you is based on what you put out into the universe, obviously.

Augustus remembered her teammates coming back from Walgreens with a copy of that *Sports Illustrated for Women* with her on the cover, but she didn't know what that would mean for her future. Not at first. All it had been was a chance to go to Tennessee, get some photos of herself taken, and meet her favorite player, Chamique Holdsclaw of the Lady Vols.

But then it dawned on her over time, from experience. She said:

Even after I saw it, I didn't get it until later on that year, [when] we played in the state championship and we lost. And the coach [who beat Augustus's team] made a comment like, "Well, maybe we should be on the front cover of *Sports Illustrated*." And that's when it hit me: *Oh, this is a really big deal. People are really taking this to heart. The way that they play against me is different.*

So now in the way that I approach games and the way that I go out and work and do things is totally different from any time before when I could just go out there and—"Oh, you lost? Well, okay, we'll do it better the next game." Like, no—you lost, and people are looking at you like they've beat the Michael Jordan of the women's game. You know what I mean? So it was different.

As *Sports Illustrated for Women*'s editor Sandy Bailey put it at the time: "She's the most exciting basketball player at this age since Cheryl Miller." No pressure, though.

But Augustus had also been trained for this. Her father, Seymore asked her at an early age what she wanted out of basketball. The Augustus family couldn't afford lessons, a fancy basketball hoop, or even a paved driveway. Seimone grew up playing on a gravel driveway, back behind their house, using a wooden basket Seymore built himself. And she remembered a day when she and her father were talking about basketball—Seimone was six or seven years old, the hot Louisiana sun beating down on them, Seimone telling her father basketball was her favorite sport. "He was like, 'You really like basketball?'" Seimone told me. "I had tried volleyball, I tried tennis. I tried golf. I tried soccer. But [there] was just something about basketball. I just had a knack for it. I just had it. He was like, 'This is something you wanna do, so you wanna be good at it or you wanna be great?' I was like, 'I wanna be great.' He was like, 'All right. Well, let's get to work.'"

Augustus said Baton Rouge wasn't really "a basketball place" when she was growing up, and certainly not for girls—she had to find her pickup games against guys, mostly. But the drills, they were all Seymore tying Seimone's right hand behind her back so she had to learn to dribble lefty, for instance. And he'd find ways to work on her game where she didn't even realize it was work. Seimone said:

> My dad is like a mastermind at figuring out ways to make me work harder. Whether it's talking trash to me or seeing how I react to criticism or stuff like that, or the creative way of getting off work and getting on a bike. Me not understanding that that's conditioning. I'm thinking I'm having a good time with my dad, and we're riding bikes. We were, but then we would stop somewhere, play a game. I would play like half an hour or however long it takes to finish a game, get back on the bike, ride somewhere else, play another game.

Augustus's identity was forged early, and it came from being what everyone around her wasn't. She was a Black woman growing up in Louisiana, in a place where the racism wasn't hard to see. In fact, she almost appreciated how open it was. She said:

> In the South, racism is very—it's out there. It's in your face, which is something you can appreciate, but then it's something that obviously annoys you at the same time, when

you see Confederate flags flying around freely. But that's just people expressing themselves. At least you know, and it's not like a hidden thing. I know that I'm in an area that I might not want to be in, and I need to move around. So it actually helps because you know what parts of town that you weren't supposed to be in, and you don't need to be in at certain times of the night [by avoiding those areas].

Then there was her sexual identity. Seimone knew from an early age that she was attracted to women, not men. She came out to her parents in her junior year of high school. Her mom was quicker to embrace her sexual identity than her dad, but ultimately she built a relationship with both of her parents based on this essential truth about herself. She was out but not in a public media way—"The people that needed to know, knew" is how she put it. Who Seimone Augustus thought needed to know would change over time.

Before the start of her junior year, her family had moved into the Capitol High School region, allowing her to play for the school her father had handpicked for her, and she was named Louisiana's Miss Basketball. As Augustus's high school coach, Alvin Stewart, told the *Journal & Courier* in December 2001: "When she gets a rebound, we no longer need a point guard. This is a kid who can shoot the three-point shot, can handle the ball like a point guard, and can rebound. There's a lot of stuff in that one package."

As Tennessee coach Pat Summitt put it: "She's one of the best offensive high school players I've seen in my career."

Seimone scored 36 points, grabbed 11 rebounds, and dished out 6 assists in the 2002 Louisiana Class 4A Championship Game, Capitol's second straight title, and repeated as Louisiana's Miss Basketball, a rare two-time winner.

She chose LSU for college over Tennessee, Rutgers, and Duke—the last where the Louisiana Miss Basketball who preceded her, Alana Beard, had picked. Then–LSU athletic director Skip Bertman called Augustus "the most important recruit in the history of our athletic program." The LSU women's basketball team averaged 1,361 fans per game the season before Seimone arrived. By the time she stepped onto the floor for her first collegiate game, LSU had sold *1,500 season tickets.*

Augustus was as advertised. She scored 27 in her debut on November 22, 2002, including 6 in OT, in a win over Arizona, adding 8 rebounds. "She is pretty good. We're going to keep her around," Gunter said after the opening-night win. She led LSU in scoring, as Sue Gunter's team reeled off 15 straight wins to begin the season; finished the regular season 24–3; dominated the SEC tournament, complete with a 78–62 drubbing of Tennessee in the Final, beating the only three teams to beat them all season along the way; and reached the Elite Eight in Augustus's freshman season.

Augustus was the only freshman on any of the All-American teams selected by the Associated Press. It wasn't simply that Augustus was living up to the billing as a great player—she was ahead of everyone else in the game.

In Seimone's sophomore season, Gunter had to step away for medical reasons during the NCAA tournament, so assistant Pokey Chatman—eventually named Gunter's successor—took over, and Augustus, who said her team wasn't ready the previous year in that Elite Eight loss to Texas, took no chances. She scored 29 all by herself, and LSU reached the Final Four with a 62–60 win over Georgia. "I've had a lot of firsts in my life, but making the Final Four ranks as one of the best," Augustus told the assembled media ahead of the 2004 national semifinal against Tennessee.

Augustus and LSU came up short against Tennessee, just as Whalen and Minnesota fell to Connecticut in the other national semifinal that season. But they both sealed their identities as saviors of their college programs, something Augustus reinforced two more times with Final Four appearances her junior and senior seasons as well, playing alongside young center Sylvia Fowles, whose name will come up again later.

And the Minnesota Lynx, after beginning the 2005 season 11–9, traded Katie Smith to the Detroit Shock in late July and finished in the lottery; these two things are not unrelated. (Also not coincidentally, the Shock were lottery-bound at the time of the deal for Smith, and ended up making the playoffs.)

Winning the lottery gave the Lynx a chance at Augustus, and they had no intention of missing that opportunity. "We'll take it and run," then–Lynx coach and Reeve's NCAA tournament nemesis Suzie McConnell-Serio said after winning the top pick. "This is big for us, for the franchise and looking forward to next year."

The Lynx made it public weeks ahead of time that they'd decided who they were going to select, and few had doubts about the identity of that draft pick. As Michael Rand put it in the *Star Tribune* on April 3, 2006: "If it's anyone except LSU's Seimone Augustus, they've overthought this thing." They hadn't.

Minnesota entrusted its future to Augustus, selecting her first overall, while utilizing the seventh pick on Shona Thorburn, the latter expected to be the team's point guard of the future alongside Augustus at shooting guard. (This did not work out, with Thorburn out of the league after 2007, creating a hole at the position that ignited cries across the fan base to bring in Whalen.) "On my evaluation form, I didn't fill out any numbers," McConnell-Serio revealed to the media on draft night. "I just wrote: 'Number one pick. No-brainer.'"

And Augustus's new teammate Tamika Williams set the bar even higher, saying of Augustus: "Right now, she is the face of women's basketball."

But while Augustus returned from a few weeks of playing for USA Basketball in a spring tour and assumed her role as leader of the Lynx, the wins did not come nearly as easily as they had when she arrived at LSU. Williams suffered a knee injury in camp and did not play up to her 2005 standard. What McConnell-Serio billed as a five-way battle for point guard minutes wasn't really won by anybody. Chandi Jones, a critical part of the return in the Katie Smith deal, was felled by a bone bruise early in camp and played in just six games all season.

A total of 9,471 people came out to watch Connecticut and a still-hobbled Whalen, coming back from surgery to repair torn ligaments in her ankle, and Augustus's debut. The rookie scored 21, but the Sun prevailed 81–69. This was the script for much of the 2006 season. Augustus scored an average of 20.3 points per game in the 24 Lynx losses. She found yet another level in the 10 wins, averaging 25.7 points per game. McConnell-Serio did not last the season with her up-tempo but defensively challenged team.

This was largely the story of Seimone Augustus and the Minnesota Lynx through the first five years of her career. In years one through three, Augustus accumulated 14.3 win shares. Only four other players had posted a higher number in the first three seasons of their WNBA careers: Cynthia Cooper, Tamika Catchings, Yolanda Griffith, and Katie Smith. Only two more, Elena Delle Donne and Maya Moore, have done so since with all but Catchings joining the WNBA after significant professional experiences elsewhere. Yet the Lynx did not have a single playoff appearance to show for it.

In 2009 the Lynx, entirely revamped around Augustus—no hold-overs at all from the 2007 team besides Seimone—won their opener over the Sky 102–85. "You know, we're tired of being in the slumps, tired of being the underestimated team in the league, or always the one at the bottom," Augustus told the Associated Press that night after 8,708 watched the Lynx. "So they made the changes to this team to one day be a contender, a team where when you're talking about the playoffs, you're talking about the Lynx."

In fact, the 2009 Lynx got off to a 4–1 start. Then Augustus tore her ACL and was lost for the season. "After the injury, the first two days, I probably cried more than I ever had cried in my life," Augustus said when she spoke to the media a few days after getting the diagnosis in 2009.

So let's take a step back and consider what Cheryl Reeve had to balance heading into 2011. No fewer than four players had a legitimate claim on the alpha dog title, with all the potential pitfalls and conflicts that went along with it: Brunson was a veteran who had actually won a championship with the Sacramento Monarchs, an All-Star, and an All-Defensive Team player. Whalen was a declared savior of the sport of women's basketball in the state of Minnesota, a hero returning home to lead the team from the point guard position with All-Star and WNBA Finals appearances on her résumé. Augustus was a declared savior of the sport of women's basketball *period*, since the age of 14, who had been the first option among her teammates at every stop, including Minnesota—the team where she'd now be asked to instead serve as one among equals. And Maya Moore, fresh off her fourth Final Four in four seasons at Connecticut—including 2 national titles and 90 consecutive victories—was the first overall pick in the 2011 WNBA Draft by acclimation.

To prepare for Moore, Reeve had consulted Whalen on player personnel moves. With Augustus, she said later, it was easy, even though Moore's arrival meant shifting positions: Augustus to shooting guard and Moore slotting in at small forward. Augustus simply was tired of losing. "There were people who reached out to Seimone and said, 'You've got to get out of Minnesota. Here comes Maya Moore. It's not going to be about you anymore,'" Reeve told ESPN.com prior to the 2015 WNBA Finals. "And Seimone scoffed and said, 'Why in the world would I not welcome help and get where I want to go with this franchise?' Seimone has been extremely loyal to the organization and to the fans."

And if Seimone Augustus wasn't worried about losing out on the credit for a turnaround to Maya Moore, well, the feeling was mutual. Moore wasn't worried about who got the spotlight. She just locked on her goals and achieved them. As a child, wanting a drum set her single mother, Kathryn, would struggle to afford, she simply decided to start her own car wash. She earned half the $400 the set cost, and Kathryn, despite the noise involved, provided the other half.

So it went, even more successfully, with a hoop Kathryn put on the door in their Jefferson City, Missouri, apartment when Maya was a child. Maya Moore recalled in her book, *Love and Justice*:

My mother didn't have grandiose aspirations when she hung the toy basketball hoop on the door of our apartment when I was only three years old. She simply needed something that could occupy my time and keep me busy while she was making dinner or doing chores. To say I was an active child is an understatement. I never stopped running or moving, whether I was inside or outside. At first, it really didn't matter what I played with—it could have been a basketball or a soccer ball or a rock—but I needed something to keep me occupied. I was a kid who loved to play.

Maya knew about the WNBA—her uncle Preston had given her a WNBA ball when she was eight years old, and she quickly began following the Houston Comets when the team debuted that summer. But her role in the league evolved in a step-by-step manner she learned from Kathryn. Maya Moore told me in 2008:

> When I was young, I had no idea I would have the moments that I've had. I was always trying to look ahead to what was right in front of me. My mom is somebody that helped me start that habit early. When I was in middle school, [she said], "Start planning ahead. What do you want to do next? What are your goals?" And she'd help me make a little middle school résumé, I remember. It was my name and my hobbies and what I liked in school, and then it eventually became bigger and bigger.
>
> I got to high school, and I would start sending college coaches my summer schedule and keeping up with the things I was achieving in the classroom. And it just always kept me focused, but I was also a very driven kid. I enjoyed achieving my goals or achieving the goals set out in front of me.

Greatness isn't about a single big swing. It's about the details. That's something Moore grasped early on. She said:

> So when I was in middle school, I was starting to dream about playing in college. Then when I got to high school, I was pretty confident I would be able to get that goal. It was just a matter of—*Keep working hard and figuring out what school to go to.*
>
> Then when I got to college, I knew if I kept on the path, the WNBA was ahead. And then I got connected with USA Basketball. Then I saw, *Wow, the Olympics are possible.* So every step I was working on the next step and hoping to get there. But it wasn't like when I was seven, when I was like, 'I'm going to be the best player ever.' I wasn't thinking that. I was just enjoying the game, having fun, and trying to figure out when I could get outside and play again.

She started sending tapes of herself playing to college coaches when she was in middle school. But by the age of 13 she had grown to 5'10", and at 14, by then in Georgia, she won her first national championship. She didn't have to send out tapes anymore, she remembered with a smile: "After that point, they knew who I was."

And to an incredibly rare extent, Moore knew who she was. Not only was she sought after in recruiting because of the ways in which she affected the game on the court, but the kind of self-motivated work ethic Moore brought to the game attracted the notice of people such as Geno Auriemma and Cheryl Reeve as well. Auriemma told the *Star Tribune* in 2011:

She came in with a tremendous reputation, with so much expected of her. She wanted to be the person others depended on. She wanted to have an impact on her teammates in every game. And she challenged herself all the time to work harder in class, on the court, and off the court.

The thing Maya does so well is she competes so hard. Her attitude, the things she does, those all rub off on the people around her—and she's able to sustain it every day.

Moore picked Connecticut over Tennessee, Duke, and Georgia. The reasons echo in what she ultimately brought to the Lynx during their championship run. She wrote:

It was an incredible opportunity to be able to choose any school that I wanted to go to. Where could I be pushed? This was the question driving me. I didn't want to go to a university where I knew I'd be the star. I wanted to go somewhere competitive, somewhere that would force me to grow and work hard. When I visited UConn and watched them practice, I knew that this was where I needed to be. It was unlike anything I'd ever seen . . . our practices were what set us apart from everybody else. What I saw that day on the court while visiting them remained true. This was the bread and butter of what made UConn, UConn. I wanted to be pushed and compete for a place and pursue greatness. They had great players and a super-competitive environment, so that was the place I wanted to put myself in.

It was also the year her godparents, Reggie and Cheri Williams, first told her about a man, Jonathan Irons, and their belief that he had been wrongly convicted of murder. That knowledge would come to define Maya Moore's life—but more on that later.

By the time she arrived in Minnesota, Moore knew what she wanted to do on the floor. And though it wouldn't blossom fully for several years, she understood the opportunity that basketball had afforded her to change the world for the better as well. "I've always been surrounded by really great people, which is a blessing," Moore said in 2011. "They helped me understand that it's not about me, that it's bigger than me. Learning that from a young age helped me have some clarity about how I need to treat this gift of being in the spotlight.

"I'm here to play basketball, to be a great basketball player. That's what I love. But that's given me the opportunity to have a voice, and I want to use it in a meaningful way."

The delight Moore felt about her circumstances—she saw the Lynx not as a team that had been bad but merely a victim of circumstances, a judgment that proved correct right away—was shared by her team-mates before she even arrived. Lynx coach Cheryl Reeve said:

> From the day we won the [draft] lottery, all the players were texting me. They were excited, because they knew who we were picking, and Maya is such a quality person. If she were selfish, it would rub people the wrong way, but she's not.
>
> Maya will handle herself so well. She is humble and mature beyond her years, and she puts so much on herself to be the best she can be. Her passion for the game, her passion for winning, those things are contagious.

And on the day the Lynx won the lottery, let there be no mistake: they were taking Moore. "In winning today's draft lottery, we are guaranteed to add someone that we expect to be an MVP-caliber player from the day she steps foot onto the court," Roger Griffith told reporters the night of the lottery in November 2010.

The Lynx had the second-best odds of getting that pick. The Tulsa Shock and Nolan Richardson had the best chance, due to their 6–28 ineptitude in 2010, but ended up with the second pick, which they used on Liz Cambage, who would have been a very different fit in Minnesota.

Even ahead of the draft, Reeve used her best "I don't want to get fined" language in discussing the imminent addition of Moore. "Well, we are on a [league] conference call, and I think if I were to confirm that, I would be in big, big trouble," Reeve said when asked flat out whether Moore was her pick. "But I will tell you that the assumptions being made are not off base and that this franchise is extremely excited about the prospect of a very talented player out of the University of Connecticut." Reeve left it to the imagination of those in the media to determine whether she meant Moore or Moore's roommate, Lorin Dixon, who'd averaged 2.9 points per game her senior season.

Ultimately, with the Lynx armed with a healthy Augustus (who'd not only rehabbed her knee fully but lost 20 pounds), Moore and fourth overall pick Amber Harris out of the draft, plus the veteran and former Detroit Shock mainstay Taj McWilliams-Franklin signed in free agency, the 2011 WNBA general manager survey was high on the team—but only relatively so. While 50 percent of GMs thought Minnesota would be the most improved team, only one GM thought they'd win the 2011 WNBA championship. "For the last few years we have been talking about, 'Oh, we need some pieces,'" Augustus said on the eve of the opener. "I feel like the pieces are here."

As Moore wrote years later:

> I was a rookie amongst greats! A lot of times high draft
> picks went to poor teams, so the rookies had a lot of
> pressure on them to take over and be the star and carry
> the team. But that's never realistic, and that's not how
> the league works. Everybody coming in needs time to
> grow and learn. That was the mindset I carried with me.
> I wanted to listen and to learn from these vets. I wanted to
> allow them to help me grow. At the same time, I wanted
> to do my job as well. I wanted to compete and do what I
> knew I could do. So entering my first year on the Lynx,
> I felt like I wasn't asked to do anything that I couldn't
> do, and that was because of the incredible veterans sur-
> rounding me.

The Lynx went out and didn't just compete, or even win; they
dominated. "We got this group together that just instantly meshed,"
Reeve said. "And training camp was incredible. The competing with
and for each other was instant. Every time we were together, it was
just really special, whether it was a shootaround, a game, in the airport,
or wherever it was. And we were on a mission."

Even when they lost, it was fuel—they dropped their opener
on the road in Los Angeles, then returned home and routed the
Sparks 86–69 in Moore's home debut. Reeve remembered how mad
McWilliams-Franklin was in the locker room about the opener ahead
of the rematch. And an early sense of how Moore handled competition at the highest level came in the second half too, after a pair of
Los Angeles threes cut Minnesota's halftime lead to 46–40.

THIS IS WHAT WE DO!

Moore stole the inbounds pass from Los Angeles to open the second half and fed Whalen for a layup. She then hit threes herself on the next two possessions. The ability to find a hinge point in the game and grab hold of it, something of a signature aspect to Moore's greatness, was obvious the very first time she performed for the Minnesota faithful. "We said we were going to get those six points back, and Maya took it personally," Reeve said following the game.

The season was like one long statement of dominance. That same week, the Lynx raced out to a 24–8 first-quarter lead against the hapless Tulsa Shock, experiencing exactly zero minutes of hell, and two days later, in Seattle, they won their first game against the Storm on the road since 2005 on the strength of a 22–0 start against Sue Bird and company. "We talk about punching the other team in the mouth," Reeve put it simply, channeling her inner Jersey and every bit of her Bill Laimbeer mentorship after going to Atlanta and routing the defending Eastern Conference champions. "When you play good defense, it makes it easier on the road."

They beat Phoenix 106–98 on July 20 to take over the lead in the Western Conference, and never relinquished it. Three days later, Moore and Brunson started in the All-Star Game, with Augustus and Whalen on the bench. Augustus heard some chirping from other All-Stars, wondering if the Lynx were for real. A few days later, they got to prove it.

Facing the San Antonio Silver Stars, who trailed the Lynx by just a game in the Western Conference standings, Minnesota found themselves down 12 at halftime. But Whalen took over in the second half, while the Lynx did what came to be a trademark—suffocating their opponents while ending possessions efficiently, finishing with a 43–28 edge on the glass. Whalen had 12 points, 4 assists, and 2 steals in the third quarter alone, and saved her best for last, a fadeaway jumper in the corner over 6'4" Jayne Appel to win it for Minnesota. Whalen recalled:

> I always love playing in San Antonio. I don't know why—maybe because of this game. We had all been All-Stars and we were having a good year. But then it was like, "Okay, what are we really going to do?"
>
> So the play was, I think, for me or Seimone, but then the ball got swung to me. And I just took one dribble and raced to get it over Jayne, who gave me the perfect guiding line with her hand. I shot over it and made it—boom, game winner.

After the celebration in the locker room, many of the players went and found their families nearby—Taj, Maya, and Monica all had family there, and Seimone's parents were in town. But not Lindsay. None of her people were there, and she had hit the game winner. So Cheryl and the coaching staff, Jim Petersen and Shelley Patterson, and trainer Chuck Barta fêted her. "We went to Pappadeaux's," Whalen said. "And it was fun because we got an Uber and we celebrated the win with a lot of adult beverages and a lot of . . . food. And it was just me and the coaches. And I just got a feeling that night of, we could really do something special."

A few weeks later, the Lynx beat the Shock 82–54 to add to their best record in the league, 18–5, and drop the Shock to 1–22. By the end of August, the Lynx clinched the top seed in the West with a 72–61 win over San Antonio. Augustus had 20; Moore had 19.

After a 7–4 start, Minnesota finished the season on a 20–3 clip, easily compiling the WNBA's best regular-season record at 27–7. The team was so balanced. They held the best net rating in the league, +10.4, on the back of second-best offensive and defensive efficiency. Augustus (16.2), Whalen (13.6), Moore (13.2), and Brunson (10.2) all averaged double figures in scoring, and none of them played even 30 minutes per game because of a deep bench featuring Wiggins, Wright, Harris, and Jessica Adair. McWilliams-Franklin, at age 40, started 33 games at center and was a stabilizing force in the middle. Everyone fit their roles precisely, even on a roster loaded with stars. Whalen, Brunson, and Augustus each won Western Conference Player of the Month honors in different months. Moore won Rookie of the Month two of three times.

And the fans started to notice too. Only 4 of the Lynx's first 10 home crowds topped 8,000 fans, but every regular-season game after August 4 did. Brunson signed a long-term contract extension that September. The displaced Monarch had found her new home.

Despite the regular-season dominance, many observers picked other teams, such as the defending champion Seattle Storm, to win in the playoffs. Reeve noticed. "We are still trying to prove the Minnesota Lynx are for real," Reeve told the *Star Tribune*. "I can kind of understand the league is pretty balanced, but when you have a six-game lead on your nearest opponent, you would think there would be a little bit more respect there. We will certainly use that with our players. But we've got to prove it."

Two Lynx figures did receive word they'd be honored as the playoffs began: Moore won Rookie of the Year, and Reeve won Coach of the Year. Asked by a reporter if she thought Roger Griffith should tear up her contract with one year remaining and provide a hefty raise, Reeve responded: "That would be a great idea."

In the Lynx's opening series against San Antonio, Whalen scored 20 and tipped away a pass with four seconds left to preserve a 66–65 Lynx victory in front of 11,891 delirious Lynx fans. The Silver Stars took Game 2, but back in Minneapolis, the Lynx got 24 from Augustus and advanced with the franchise's first-ever playoff series win, 85–67. Afterward the team danced on the court, as they always did after wins, Moore yelling, "We're not finished yet!"

San Antonio would be the only team to notch so much as a playoff win against the 2011 Minnesota Lynx. In both Minnesota's WNBA Finals games at Target Center, more than 15,000 fans poured through the turnstiles. Remembering how she felt prior to Game 1 of the 2011 WNBA Finals, Knox said:

> Honestly, [it's not] the actual winning of the game; it's that moment before the clock ever starts for the game where I walk in . . . and I see a sold-out arena and one of the biggest crowds ever in the history of the WNBA. For me, that is my championship. That is my moment in my career. I'm like, "Oh my God, look at all these people and what we were able to accomplish together." All these people are getting it, that they're a part of this movement. It is every time those moments happen to me, and I remember in 2011 vividly that we did this. We did this together. We created this. We are all a part of something bigger than whatever happens on the court in that Game 5. To me, that's my championship moment where I'm like, "Wow."

The line to buy tickets to Game 1 stretched all the way out the Target Center and down First Avenue. All 1,000 playoff T-shirts sold out, and 600 people signed up for 2012 season tickets that day alone. And it was all chronicled in an A1 story in the *Star Tribune*.

The one way the 2011 Minnesota Lynx failed their fans was by sweeping the Atlanta Dream 3–0, meaning that the clincher came on the road. (It was a favor to much of Maya Moore's family, who lived in Georgia.) Seimone Augustus, whose Game 2 performance was one of the best in Finals history (36 points on 14 shots from the field), won Finals MVP. Those around her who said she should leave Minnesota due to Maya Moore's arrival had been silenced.

And despite the road clinching, Minneapolis was still well prepared to celebrate their Lynx. Watch parties had been set up all over the city, and the Lynx headed to a club in Atlanta before taking an early flight home the next morning.

Whalen remembers a *little* from that time. Only in later years did she get wise to the strategy of getting to bed somewhat early on a title-winning night—"Midnight, like Cinderella, is the magic number," she said—so she could properly enjoy the crowd of supporters at the airport when she and the team returned to Minnesota, the parade to follow. She got a lot of practice.

"Yeah, that parade was crazy," Whalen recalled. "And I was just like—'Oh, man, this is stuff you dream of.' Like, filling the streets. And packing downtown. People just can't go anywhere. People are just all over, you know—just pictures, autographs, and all celebrating."

Another 15,000 people showed up for the parade on October 11 down Seventh Avenue to the Target Center, cheering, waving alongside the Mary Tyler Moore statue, and the Lynx were celebrated properly. The weather even cooperated somehow—it was 69 degrees in Minnesota in October. Reeve turned to Roger Griffith in the white Lexus slowly making its way along the parade route and asked him: "You never dreamt it could be like this, right?"

Ten days later, Cheryl Reeve and Carley Knox were married. The championship was not only exhilarating for them both but healing, too. "I would say that for each ring that we've won, starting with 2011, the pain of what happened in Detroit was eased a little bit more," Knox said. "Every ring helped me forget a little bit more." Of course, without the Detroit Shock and its impractically placed fax machine, there would have been no wedding rings, either.

Ever the planner, Reeve thought the date, October 21, 2011, would allow players who had to head overseas once the WNBA season ended. And so many did, Knox recalled, the friends and family of the couple who had built a championship team together gathering at the Calhoun Beach Club, which overlooks Lake Calhoun and is just a three-mile drive from the Target Center in downtown Minneapolis. "That's the great thing," Knox said in 2018 of how much of their WNBA family was there to celebrate them together. "[It was] 14 years in the WNBA for me and obviously a lot longer for Cheryl. [Make that 20 years for Knox and 23 years for Reeve as the book goes to press.] We're in it together and we've remained very close with a number of these players that we just share the same passion."

And with that, the two of them took off for a honeymoon in Hawaii, starting a family tradition: every time the Lynx win a title, they return to the Aloha State.

But neither Knox nor Reeve was satisfied in 2011. The overall rise in attendance was encouraging, but there was much more to do. And

Reeve had a message for her players once the parade reached Target Center: "In your championship runs, you have a window. You have a combination of young players and older players, and you maximize that. For us, it looks like we should be good for a little while longer." The Lynx, and their battles on and off the court, were just getting started.

On January 23, 2012, the Lynx announced the re-signing of Taj McWilliams-Franklin, as sure a sign of team happiness as any. McWilliams-Franklin was 41 and had the chance to ride off into the sunset having won a title. But as she explained, she "wanted to do it all again."

Jessica Adair and Candice Wiggins returned as well, joining Taj, as the Lynx looked to simply run it back, though they did add shooter Erin Thorn via free agency and drafted Devereaux Peters with the third overall pick (the Lynx had a knack for convincing other teams to trade them lottery picks in exchange for ancillary players in those days).

Reeve understood there'd be no sneaking up on teams as the season began. "That's what you want," she told the AP on the eve of the 2012 season. "We wanted to walk in here saying we were the best team. We earned that right."

While it was a quiet off-season for the Lynx, Minnesota itself saw a resurgence in women's basketball, thanks to the arrival of a player who has come to own so many records in the Gophers' books to this day: Rachel Banham. And to understand how far the game had come since Lindsay Whalen, along with how far it still had to travel, it is useful to understand Banham's path.

Like Whalen, Banham had attended a high school outside the Twin Cities limits. It was a half hour drive from Lakeville North High School, Banham's alma mater, to Williams Arena. But Banham knew, growing up, that she wanted to play professional basketball in a way Whalen didn't. And she had a template because of Whalen: to excel in high school, to play for the University of Minnesota, and to make it to the Minnesota Lynx, a team she'd latched on to even before Whalen returned home. "Somehow I loved them just as much even when they were losing," Banham said. Don and Mel, Rachel's parents—both Minneapolis police officers—bought Rachel a custom BANHAM Lynx jersey that would turn out to be prophetic.

Her brothers, Cole (one year older) and Blake (three years younger), never took it easy on Rachel, and she found that her ability to hold her own with them in driveway games gave her early confidence in her path. "We played every sport together: football, basketball, baseball—like anything my parents threw at us, we just loved," Banham told me in 2022, the two of us sitting in her office at the University of Minnesota. "We just love sports. We still do to this day. And we were very competitive, as you can imagine. So being the sister, they always wanted to pick on me, and of course I wanted to beat them. So I think my parents knew from a young age I was just a really good athlete, and basketball was my thing. It was just natural for me."

Banham still has that Lynx jersey. It doesn't fit—which is fine, as she can just wear her actual, grown-up ones now—but it dates back to the time she first came to understand basketball didn't have to just be a passion for her; it could be a destination. It was tangible in a way Peps Neuman never had, and Whalen had to create herself. When Whalen was 10, there was no WNBA.

"It's weird to think back on it, but fourth grade is when I very much remember I was a step above the rest," Banham said. "*Yes, I love this.* Like I was so passionate about it. And my parents were like, 'All right, do it.' I've spent hours in the gym and on the driveway, and they're all for it—you know, you want the kids out of the house. But school is—I mean, I always say get your degree all that stuff—but school I wasn't super passionate about. I was like, 'I want to ball.'"

And ball she did—for her school teams, for AAU teams—and the rest of the country took notice. There would be no delay for Pam Borton's staff to recruit the preternatural shooter and playmaker a short drive from campus, but Borton was far from alone. Lisa Bluder and Iowa were in early on Banham too. So was most of the Big Ten, Banham remembers. Even UConn, late in the process, sent a letter after her AAU summer junior year of high school, when she was elevated to a top 20 recruit in the country, something she remembered was "kind of sick" at the time it happened.

But by then she'd already committed to the U. And just as the level of attention grew exponentially compared to Whalen, it is also worth noticing the difference between Banham's level of recruiting and the no-holds-barred way the entire country's best NCAA programs pursued the Banham of a few years later: Paige Bueckers of Hopkins High School. "We both were from big suburbs," Banham said. "Okay. And we both played for 4A schools, both played in the state tournament. . . . Our team was really good, but their team was really, *really* good. They were stacked. And obviously Paige is incredible, but I think the biggest difference is social media. You see all these highlights of people doing sick passes that you didn't [during my time]; you weren't gonna get any of that when I was playing."

Banham remembered Twitter becoming a thing people knew about when she was a senior at Lakeville North. Instagram didn't even launch until her senior year. I mentioned to her that I had people sending me highlights of Bueckers from her freshman year of high school, and Banham joked, "Right, and what were they going to do, send you a DVD of me?"

The speed with which social media changed everyone's ability to see players has been a critical development in the women's game, according to Banham. "I was like, 'What is this? This is a stupid, right?'" Banham said of Instagram, where she created an account her freshman year of college. "So like, think about that in high school, when you have all these kids' highlights you can see, like I'm seeing all these kids' highlights . . . too. *She's good. Where's she going?* I'm looking right, of course; I follow and see all their highlights. We didn't have that during my time. So it makes a difference."

Banham was a prodigy on par with Whalen, starting to play varsity at Lakeville North in eighth grade. In ways it took time for the state to know what it had in Whalen, it didn't with Banham, who won Minnesota Associated Press High School Player of the Year her senior season of high school, an award Whalen didn't win. In many ways, Banham was like if you took a computerized version of Whalen and looked to make her even better. Banham was 5'9" but had a stronger frame earlier on. She could shoot the three more, and more efficiently, than Whalen could. She felt like the natural evolution of the women's game.

By the time Banham arrived at Minnesota, head coach Pam Borton put the program into her hands, making her the starting point guard on day one, just as Whalen had been a decade earlier. And make no mistake: the entire program's future rested on Banham. Just take this description from the October 13, 2011, *Star Tribune*—before Banham had played a single varsity game:

> Pam Borton is able to encapsulate her Gophers' coaching tenure with a sweep of her right hand. Starting near her chin, her hand descends to a belt-top valley and then, ever so slightly, rises again.
>
> The final upward movement is based more on her personal faith in this year's team than recent results. . . .
>
> The single biggest reason for hope rests on an unlikely source—freshman point guard Rachel Banham—given that most college coaches value experience at the position. But Banham is a precocious youngster who offers intriguing potential.

Banham was, of course, compared to Whalen, both by Borton and by the writer of the piece. She didn't shy away from it.

"I think it's cool, because I watched her play," Banham said that day. "She's incredible. For someone to say that, it's an honor. That's a lot to live up to, but that's my goal. I want to do what she did for the team."

A double-edged sword, sure, but one Banham embraced right away. Borton called her the motor that drives the engine the next four seasons. "There's pressure," Banham said. "But it's good pressure."

Borton, meanwhile, had the luxury of a long-term contract—one that ran through 2014 and was finally closer to market rate for Big Ten coaches at $405,000 per season, with a $1 million buyout. Ultimately Banham and Borton needed to turn around both the fortunes of the team on the floor and find a way to bring fans back to Williams Arena, where attendance for the women's games had fallen from 9,703 fans per game in the Whalen Final Four season of 2003–04 to 3,540 the year before Banham arrived.

That didn't change overnight, though the results did improve—the Gophers finished 19–17 in 2011–12 and 6–10 in the Big Ten, after a 12–18, 4–12 campaign the year before Banham arrived. And given the chance to play in a postseason tournament, the Women's Basketball Invitational (WBI)—essentially the bronze medal of postseason tournaments after the NCAA and WNIT—the Gophers went out and won it, beating Northern Iowa 88–74 in the title game right at Williams Arena. Banham had 26 on 14 shots, plus 4 rebounds and 4 assists. It was the first winning season for U of M since 2008–09. "I think it's just sweet that we ended up in a championship," Banham said. "That's what our seniors needed, and I think it's really good for the program."

But it's hard to say the Gophers were resonating again the way they had during the Whalen years—though, to be clear, if the direct comparison is the Whalen years, that Minnesota team won a just single Big Ten game her freshman season and didn't even play at Williams Arena. Even so, the listed attendance for Banham and the Gophers at the WBI championship was just 1,300. There was more work to do.

But Banham was everything Minnesota could have asked for and more. She captured Big Ten Freshman of the Year honors, scored 16.1 points per game, hit 42.5 percent of her threes on 3.5 attempts per game, and elevated the Gophers beyond what the undersized roster had any right to accomplish. She brought none of the inconsistency one normally associates with a freshman, scoring in double figures 33 of 36 games, and 20 or more nine times.

And then it almost all ended as swiftly as it began. During a summer game, Rachel felt weak, and knew something was wrong. She and her parents went to a doctor, and Banham spent several nights in the hospital as tests eventually diagnosed her with a pulmonary embolism, or, in layman's terms, a blood clot in her lungs. As friends and family, Borton, and her teammates visited, Banham's mind went to the place it always does first: the game. She said:

> I just started crying and I didn't even know what that meant. I was like, "Can I play basketball?" And that's all I could talk about was like, "When can I play basketball again?" And he was like, "Well, we need to sit and talk," and I just could not stop crying. That was like the only thing I could think: *I can't play basketball.* And he was like, "You can't play for three months." I had to be on blood thinners, and you can't play when you're on blood thinners. And I was devastated because this was my sophomore year in college. So I [was] still young. And you know, I [loved] the game and I [had] to sit out.

Eventually, she got clearance to do some noncontact work, but though she'd earned All–Big Ten first-team preseason honors, she still didn't get cleared for contact until the day before Minnesota's first exhibition game, at home against Concordia–St. Paul. Do you think Banham was excited to be back? She scored 22 points in 28 minutes and sank both of her three-point attempts.

Banham's sophomore year built on her freshman campaign in virtually every measurable way. She averaged 20.7 points per game, dramatically improved her midrange and ability to get to the rim—from

41.8 percent from two to 48 percent from two—and increased her assist percentage from 18.5 to 26.5, while lowering her turnover percentage from 16.7 to 12.8. She was among the most dangerous scorers in the Big Ten once more, and a significantly more efficient playmaker as well.

But it was a summer of battles for many. The Lynx had everyone coming at them, and not just on the court as defending champions. The state of Minnesota was coming for their basic human rights. Seimone Augustus could still remember walking through the halls of her high school, hearing the whispers: "She's gay, she's gay." When she got to Minnesota, she felt like she'd come to a "big melting pot" and felt welcomed, even more so when she met LaTaya Varner at a club. The two were inseparable after that, and LaTaya helped Seimone through the darkest days of losing and injuries with the Lynx.

So in December 2010, while Seimone and LaTaya were on the beach in Miami, Augustus made her big decision. She wrote in 2015:

> I'd arranged for two sandcastles to be built on the beach, with a ribbon going through. We walked down to the sand at sunset, and there was a small crowd forming around the sculptures. "Why don't you go see what's going on?" I told her. While she walked towards the sculptures, I pulled the ring out of my pocket. She turned back and saw me with the ring. She started to cry. An older woman in the crowd asked, "Well, what did she say?" She said yes.

A long engagement followed, LaTaya planning a wedding at either the Walker Art Center in Minnesota or back in her home state of Hawaii in the spring of 2013. But then Republicans in the Minnesota state legislature voted in the spring of 2011 to put a constitutional amendment on the ballot in Minnesota, to be voted on in November 2012, reading: "Only a union of one man and one woman shall be valid or recognized as a marriage in Minnesota." Suddenly the legal framework of both Augustus's plans and the marriage of Knox and Reeve were in significant peril.

But the foundation the Lynx had built made room for more than just a successful basketball team. A critical reason the Lynx have come to embody progress in the Twin Cities is through Knox's marriage of the personal and the political within supporters of the team. Knox said:

> We are doing that here in Minnesota, and that's something that I'm so proud of. We are, year after year, the most profitable team in the WNBA. Yeah, we still have room to grow, but the fact that we're trying to lift up the rest of the WNBA and all the teams and show the world what is possible in women's athletics and that people are watching and they do care and they are going to pay, whether it be for tickets or corporate sponsorship or President's Circle. That's something I most proud of.

So it was a natural enough fit to support Seimone when she decided to move from a framework Cheryl had used throughout her professional career—"those who needed to know, knew" about her sexuality—to becoming a public advocate to vote no on Prop 1, the place on the ballot where Minnesotans would decide whether or not to ban gay marriage in the state constitution.

Seimone had always been politically aware, she said, particularly about LGBTQ+ issues. Making that leap to public advocacy was a different story. "But when the time came around with the whole marriage equality thing here in Minnesota—up until that point, you can trace the track record," Augustus told me in 2018. "Like, I hadn't done anything. I had never used my platform, never really spoke out and said anything. And that was something that was near and dear to me. At the time, I was in—I thought—a great situation, and I wanted to show what a beautiful gay couple looks like. I thought that that was an example I wanted to put out there."

The panic never made any sense to Augustus. She remembered parents approaching her in high school, telling her she'd made their daughters question their sexuality, too. Now all these years later, it was happening again, in a state she'd considered a safe place for herself. "I just never understood why someone else's love life and who they love and who they choose to be with affects so many other people's lives," Augustus said that fall, as the vote approached. "Is it a scare of, 'Gay people are going to be running around and everyone's going to turn gay?' I never understood the whole point of opposing or hating someone else's happiness."

Though Lynx owner Glen Taylor, a moderate Republican, has given money to politicians throughout his life who oppose gay marriage, both Cheryl and Carley have spoken at length about the ways in which Taylor has never wavered from supporting the Lynx, both in a basketball sense and beyond. But it was a tightrope just the same. Cheryl, in her official bio on the Lynx site, didn't yet mention Carley back in 2012. But she did speak out in support of Seimone at the time. "The easier route would be to stay closeted because it isn't as accepted as we hope it would be," Lynx coach Cheryl Reeve said during the 2012 WNBA Finals. "I'm really proud of her for being out in the forefront."

No, the Lynx didn't repeat. The great Tamika Catchings captured her first WNBA championship, the Indiana Fever defeating a heavily favored Minnesota team in four games. But reflecting on the loss that night in Indiana, Reeve noted, "There's not anybody that cannot be happy for Tamika Catchings to finally get a championship," and she was already looking ahead to 2013. Reeve said from the podium:

> You know, Candice Wiggins said this early in the season: the hungry lion hunts best. And I think for us we had our challenges with the idea of being hungrier than the teams that we were playing. Once you have something, it's human nature to not be as hungry as someone else who doesn't have it. So we really tried to battle through that most of the season, and I thought we did a really nice job of that. We overcame a number of scenarios where I thought we were really trying to find that place that was wanting it more than our opponent, which was hard to do.
>
> We overcame a lot this season. It was very, very challenging from the word *go* for us in training camp. Training camp was different for us. We didn't have everybody there. We kind of got the trickle-in thing, so I didn't get that chemistry with the first five that I had in 2011, not to say that these guys—these guys are terrific; they've won 54 games in 2 years. . . .
>
> I've got a group—I've got a starting five that obviously we did a lot of great things with. Every year you have changes, but there's no question that you've got Lindsay, Seimone, Maya, and Rebekkah Brunson, who's in her prime.

For me everything is around them. That's how we go. So yeah, we've got the blueprint that we mapped out prior to 2011, the group that we have, the way that we play, and I think now that something was taken away from us and we're no longer defending champs, it'll be nice to kind of start fresh and see if we can't keep this thing going.

Still, the big-picture wins kept coming. The 2011 Lynx's average attendance of 8,447 had been the highest since the team's inaugural year in 1998. Well, in 2012, that had jumped to 9,683 per game, a 14.6 percent leap, and all the way up to second in the WNBA, behind only Los Angeles.

And love won on the ballot, narrowly—51.9 to 48.1 percent. There was still a law against gay marriage on the books in Minnesota, but it was ultimately rendered moot too, thanks to the Supreme Court's ruling in *Obergefell v. Hodges*. "It worked," Augustus told me in 2018. "I'm not saying I'm the sole reason why, but it gave people something like, 'Oh, okay, they're a really nice couple, and they're really super cool,' or whatever it was that clicked for some people here in Minnesota."

Augustus learned from the experience that the organization had her back. She learned too from the outpouring of support she received for speaking out. "But you get so many people reaching out, like, 'Oh, my God, I'm glad you said it because I've been living with this for 15, 20 years,'" she told me. "And it just takes someone that they see that, like you said, they can relate to, that's in a position of power. They normally don't expect us to speak out because it's not our job or whatever, and people might think [ill of us]." She filed that information away, as did her teammates. The chance to change the world would come up again.

And the Lynx took the suggestion of that *Star Tribune* reporter in December 2012, signing Reeve to a big new contract extension. Carley got a promotion too, that November, to director of business operations. And the two of them made a big decision: to start to try to have a child together.

For Reeve, 2013 was about resurrecting old partnerships and championships. She knew she'd created something special when, that winter, after a 27–7 season and trip to the Finals, people would approach her in the grocery store not with congratulations—or worse, indifference—but a simple question: "What happened?" That's where the expectations were for the Lynx now.

The Lynx built around their core, forced to find a new starting center after Taj McWilliams-Franklin called it quits at the tender age of 41. So they sent Candice Wiggins to Tulsa in exchange for the rights to Janel McCarville, who'd been plying her trade overseas since 2010.

Eventually, after Reeve flew to Turkey and convinced her, McCarville took the chance to play one state over from her native Wisconsin and Reeve had a starting center. McCarville had learned the game Peps Neuman–style, on a homemade hoop her father, Terry, built himself on the family chicken coop in Stevens Point, Wisconsin. Reeve plugged the hole created by the loss of Wiggins's offense by snagging Sugar Rodgers with the 14th pick, part of an evolving tradition for the Lynx of scoring well with later picks, the consequence of their on-court success.

It all worked as planned. The Lynx raced out to a 7–3 start in 2013, then got even better, winning 10 in a row and finishing at 26–8. Once again, they had the best net rating in the WNBA, reflecting a top offense and defense. And once again they led the league in rebounding percentage.

The playoffs were merely a coronation. Minnesota won all seven games, sweeping Tina Thompson's Storm, Brittney Griner's Mercury, and Angel McCoughtry's Dream, winning by an average of 15.4 points per game. Another parade followed. Another trip to Hawaii for Carley and Cheryl. Whalen and Augustus signed contract extensions. The Lynx, for all their dominance, had the second-youngest roster in the league.

As Seimone yelled into the microphone the day of the celebration at the Target Center following the parade: "This is what we do!"

The following summer, the Lynx visited the White House. Again. "When the Lynx were here in 2012, I told them I had a feeling they'd be back," President Barack Obama said. "I just want to mention I was right. You can fact-check that, PolitiFact." Obama also noted that between her UConn days, USA Basketball gold medal in the 2012 Olympics, a pickup game with the president, and the Lynx titles, this was Maya Moore's sixth visit to 1600 Pennsylvania Avenue. "Basically, there's like a Maya Moore wing in the White House," Obama said. "We've got all her stuff here. She's got a toothbrush."

It was, of course, Cheryl's fourth visit—two with the Shock, two with the Lynx. She had a strategy by then too for how to navigate such moments. "More than anything, soak up the moment, enjoy it with each other, and make sure you take a lot of pictures," Reeve told Minnpost.com.

Reeve's perspective was also born of a newfound sense of how quickly it all can change. In January 2014 Reeve attempted to work out, but her legs felt heavy and she had to stop after just a few minutes. She resolved that if it didn't get better, she'd get it checked out. But of course it was the height of college-evaluation and free-agency-preparation season, so she didn't.

But as February turned into March, she found herself with tingling and numbness in her toes as well. Finally, in late March, she went to the doctor, and found out the frightening news: a meningioma, a mass on her spine, had formed. Just a few years after she'd lost her father to cancer, she feared the worst. Surgery was scheduled immediately, and fortunately, the tumor was benign. Her mother and brothers flew in for the early April surgery, and good thing, since there were complications, including an infection, and eventually a spinal drip. She was forced to spend draft night in her hospital bed, Skyping into the draft room.

To complicate matters further, the two years she and Carley had been trying to have a child finally led to Carley's getting pregnant at, essentially, the exact same time. (Ollie was born in November 2014, if you'd like to do the math.) "She kept going, 'Check again. Check again,'" Knox recalled to me in 2018, laughing. "I had like 30 pee sticks lying around. It's ironic the way life works out. It's such an incredible celebratory moment, and at the same time we were just finding out at the exact same time what was going on with her medically, which [was] really scary."

Ultimately 2014 stands out as the year of recovery. Monica Wright had knee surgery in training camp. Peters and Brunson both had off-season knee surgeries—Brunson only played in 11 games in 2014, costing the Lynx their most important interior presence. Augustus missed eight games due to bursitis in her left knee. Maya Moore had the best scoring season of her career, averaging 23.9 points per game and winning WNBA MVP honors, but a big reason why was that she had to—this was one of only two seasons between 2011 and 2017 the Lynx weren't atop the league in net rating.

But Reeve saw no particular reason to change course in her post-season interviews after the Lynx were eliminated by Brittney Griner. "Healthy is a big thing in this league," she told the *Star Tribune*'s Kent Youngblood. The one thing she was hoping to do, she said? Get a little bigger. "We've gotten away with being a little small," Reeve said. "That might be something we could look at." That's what they call foreshadowing.

And in case she needed any further reinforcement that her core was ready to keep on winning, Moore, Augustus, and Whalen all starred on the USA Basketball World Championship gold medal team that fall in Turkey, with Reeve getting a close look as an assistant under head coach Geno Auriemma. "It's always special to celebrate with them," Whalen recalled. "We got a picture together right away."

The Lynx continued to draw too, with regular-season attendance in both 2013 and 2014 well over 9,000 per game, second in the WNBA each year but trailing different teams. The Lynx were fast becoming the constant, the standard, off the court as well. Not just popular but profitable.

And then, in November, came Ollie Knox-Reeve. Carley remembered years later:

The day he was born it was amazing. I went through some stuff medically through that, but he was safe for the whole time, which was great. The greatest thing I've ever done in my life, and I believe that we've ever done in our life. He's just so incredible and so loving and kind and a wonderful leader and just so funny and sarcastic at the same time. He's incredible. I think Cheryl would tell you the same thing—that we've never loved anything more than Oliver. He just makes my life so rich and full, and I'm so proud of him every single day—in the young boy that he is and the young man that I'm watching him become.

Over in Williams Arena, Banham and the Gophers were reaching new heights, but not enough people were coming to see it. Swedish import Amanda Zahui B. took over at center, and the 6'5" pick-and-pop master immediately punished defenses who concentrated too much on Banham. But even when double-teamed, Banham was increasingly unstoppable, scoring at a clip of 22.1 points per game in her junior season and making an incredible 42.1 percent of her threes on 6.5 attempts per contest. But the Gophers never did find a reliable third scorer, and despite winning six of eight Big Ten games down the stretch, they finished 22–13, 8–8 in conference, good enough for the NIT. They even hosted a pair of those NIT games at home—crowds each time were fewer than a thousand. Borton's contract was bought out, and the Gophers hired Marlene Stollings away from Virginia Commonwealth University. Stollings agreed to a $425,000 salary, less per year to start than Borton had been making. Stollings promised an offense-first attack, music to Banham's ears. "I was blessed to have them as my coaches, but I'm also super excited for the opportunity for something different," Banham told the *Star Tribune* in April 2014. "I love that she's offensive-minded, because I think that we all know I love offense."

Stollings led the Gophers to the NCAA tournament in 2014–15, despite losing Banham—the preseason Big Ten Player of the Year— 10 games into the season with a torn ACL, and fellow Minnesota native Carlie Wagner picked up the scoring load from the perimeter. (Wagner patterned her game after Banham as surely as Banham patterned hers after Whalen.) The offensive rating jumped from 107th to 67th nationally. The defensive rating dropped from 144th in Borton's final season to 264th in Stollings's first campaign. By 2015–16 the offensive rating was 15th in the country, with a fully recovered Banham, the defensive rating was 338th out of 349 Division I teams, and the Gophers were back in the NIT.

Banham's injury—which extended her career to a fifth season after she was granted a redshirt season and returned—also shaped the way she thought about her basketball future. "When I tore my ACL is when I was really thinking about coaching," Banham told me. "Our coach at the time was like, 'You can be an extension of us—think like you're a coach,' and I was like, 'Okay,' and that's when I was like, 'Oh, this is different over here on the sideline,' and started seeing things from a different angle. So I feel like my senior year is when I actually took it seriously." So while playing was Banham's next step, she came to understand that she wanted a role as a coach someday as well, an idea she hasn't let go of since.

As 2015 dawned, the WNBA was not enjoying the same renaissance league-wide that the Lynx were experiencing at home. While attendance was strong in Minnesota, the league saw its average numbers dip throughout the first half of the 2010s. By 2015 it hit a season low of just 7,318 per game for the league. The discussions around the league were almost all negative. Diana Taurasi took a bonus from her Russian team, UMMC Ekaterinburg, to rest during the summer instead of play. The stories focused on how much she made for Ekat—$1.5 million—and how much the Mercury were going to pay her—$107,000.

Meanwhile, in the largest media market, James Dolan and Isiah Thomas combined to concoct the kind of scheme that only James Dolan would think was a good idea. Despite Thomas having been found liable for sexually harassing Anucha Browne, costing Dolan's parent company $11.6 million, Dolan installed Thomas as team president of a women's basketball team, the New York Liberty, and attempted to give him an ownership stake as well. The league could not prevent Dolan from hiring Thomas, but it could, through the ownership committee, prevent Thomas from getting a slice of the team. Sufficiently rankled, Dolan ultimately decided to announce he was selling the Liberty without having found a buyer, and moved them immediately from Madison Square Garden to the Westchester County Center in White Plains, New York, at least a 40-minute drive from the team's fans to an arena that charitably seated 3,000 and ultimately was deemed insufficiently kept up to host even high school basketball tournaments just a few years later.

But Reeve was undaunted by the prospect of a WNBA season without Taurasi—in fact, it cleared a path for the Lynx to return to the WNBA Finals, though she remained confident that her Lynx, healthy, could beat anyone.

The Lynx added international talent that off-season with the addition of Spanish point guard Anna Cruz, in a draft day trade with the New York Liberty, who selected Kiah Stokes with the 11th overall pick they received in return. Reeve wanted the Lynx to get bigger. What was she holding out for?

On April 28, 2015, that answer started appearing in public view. "Sylvia Fowles has been one of the most recognizable names in the WNBA and a face that has been intertwined with the identity of the [Chicago] Sky, but 'Big Syl' appears ready to move on," the *Chicago Tribune* reported on April 28. "The three-time All-Star has requested a trade, the team said Monday. Head coach and general manager Pokey Chatman said Fowles has a specific team in mind but declined to identify the franchise as the team explores options."

Chatman also revealed that the two teams had exchanged proposals over the past several months. Both Reeve and Griffith had managed to get lottery picks from other teams without the added leverage of being the only game in town, so they were not inclined to give up much. Chatman, naturally, wanted more of a return for her most important player other than Elena Delle Donne. The two teams faced a stalemate that reached well into the regular season.

To understand why Sylvia Fowles wanted to join the Lynx, it is necessary to understand who Sylvia Fowles is. Sylvia was born in Miami, Florida, on October 6, 1985, the youngest of five children. She was raised by her mom, Arittio (though everyone calls her Loretta), and her "mom-mom," Dorothy. When Sylvia was five, Dorothy passed, and the family of six moved into the projects, called the 40s because of the blocks they occupied in Miami. Sylvia remembers what it felt like to be a Black child in America. She told me in 2018:

When we used to go to the store, people put you in categories. If you automatically went into a store, their first thing is, you're coming here to steal. Normally, we used to go to certain stores. They were like, "All right, two of y'all can only come in at one time." It's like, "Really? You really think we're gonna steal your stuff?" I was too scared to steal 'cause my mom was gonna beat us. I was like, "I ain't got time to be stealing." That's the one thing she always taught us: never start a fight and never take something that's not ours.

Sylvia wasn't serious about basketball through the end of middle school, and that was just fine by Loretta. Sylvia said:

My mother's never been sports-savvy. She was all about academics. She couldn't have cared less about what we did with sports. Growing up, it was hard because she always worked. She never wanted to come to games when she did have off days, and it's like, "Why don't you just come?" She was like, "Your homework done?"

She never really cared about sports, and I think that's what pushed me harder, because it's like, "I'm gonna show her. I'm committed to this. This is what I want to do." She used to always say, "Don't waste your time if you're not gonna be determined to be what it takes."

For Fowles, she really began to pop as a prospect in ninth grade, when she grew suddenly to 6'3". And she got some extra attention with an athletic feat on February 15, 2001, that simply wasn't something any high school players in Florida girls' basketball had ever done: dunking a basketball. Fowles remembered:

I started dunking with a volleyball in eighth grade, actually. Once I got in high school, all the mechanics just started pulling together. You have people to teach you the proper mechanics and how to do this, how to do that, and then it was probably a couple games within the season, and they [were] like, "Look, this is the play we're gonna run. Sylvia, all we need you to do is just run, and our guard is gonna give it to you."

Up until that moment, I had a lot of jitters. You're only in ninth grade. It's like, "What if I miss? I don't wanna miss in front of all these people." We used to have really good crowds at our high school games, so . . . Then it's like, "All right, just let flow." As the game went on, Coach was saying, "You ready?" I'm like, "No."

All I can just remember is focusing, like, "All right, this is what you do. When we get the rebound, you run to this spot," and I was being very specific. "You run to this spot. When you get it, make sure you bounce. Don't travel." [There were] all these things going through my head at that moment, and then I can just remember the ball coming to me, and I was like, "I got it. I got it." Everything just went out the window. All my fear, all my anxiety, and I'm just remembering just getting to taking my two dribbles and then my one-two steps, and it was a dunk, and then two possessions later, I did it again. I just felt comfortable.

The newspapers were still talking about it weeks later, with the *Miami Herald* explaining that fans around the state were rooting for Edison High to reach the state Final Four so "everybody can see that girl who dunks from Miami."

Feeling comfortable is very, very important to Sylvia Fowles. The amount of media attention she got from the two dunks was outsized, and she started hearing from collegiate programs all over the country. But for her, the path forward wasn't fame, or travel. It was much simpler than that. She'd watched Loretta work at many jobs to make ends meet for their family—security guard, warehouse stocking, aide at a senior center—and wanted to figure out a way to do something that would mean her mother never had to work again. Fowles said:

> I think once I got past that hump in ninth grade with my coaches and everything else, and I'd seen how I progressed from year to year, I was like, "This is something I wanna do—not just for me but something to give back to my mom." She worked hard. She provided for five kids. She was the only parent. I was like, "What can be my reward to give back to my mom?" I think that's what changed my mindset. I'm like, "Okay, if I can do A, B, and C, I can get into college. At some point, I can possibly make it to the WNBA." But I never took their perspective, dang, I would be on the USA team. I'd be traveling overseas. That picture was way beyond my imagination, honestly. I think my basic mindset was, "How can I be in a place where I can provide for my family at a comfortable rate, where Mom [doesn't] have to work anymore?" That was my mindset.

Edison reached the Final Four, and ultimately the state championship, beating Winter Springs 65–56. And Fowles did a lot more than just dunk. She had 12 points, 6 rebounds, 6 blocks, and made the All-Tournament team as a freshman. "That big girl was getting rebounds over four of us," Winter Springs' Missy Guadagnino said after the game. "We tried to box her out, but she was like Shaq." And so began a lifelong ability to get the rebound—one that eventually landed Sylvia atop the all-time leaderboard for the WNBA in rebounding.

Scholanda Dorrell and Florence Williams both graduated from that Edison High team and headed to LSU, but Fowles had three years of high school left, with some in and around Miami wondering if she'd jump directly from high school to the WNBA, having grown another inch over the summer, to 6'4". "That's too much garbage to think about now," her high school coach, Denise Novak, told the *Miami Herald* in November 2001. "We are taking it slow with her. Last year her role was just to get up and down the court and to rebound. Any points were gravy. This year we are looking for her to score more points and to develop a lot from the left side. Like Shaq, she needs to work on her free throws, but she is improving. She understands that teams are going to make her prove she can make the free throws before they leave her alone underneath."

She even had company in the high school dunking department by the following season—a 6'3" sophomore from Naperville, Illinois, named Candace Parker dunked in a game as well.

Fowles did manage to figure out how to score—20.6 per game her sophomore season—leading Edison to another state title and finishing with 32 points, 21 rebounds, and 6 blocks in the 6A championship game. "Fowles is special. What can I say?" Novak said of her star center after the game. "I just thank God she is with us for two more years."

But Novak had only one more year, then was fired after what was reportedly a disagreement with her school principal. That cost Edison

Fowles too; she transferred to a private school, Gulliver, which was overjoyed to have her.

By the time Fowles arrived on the LSU campus, there was a comfort factor that helped her pick it over Connecticut and Florida State, the other two finalists for her services. Seimone Augustus welcomed her. Her former teammates, Dorrell and Williams, were on hand. She found her place, and easily. (Her mom even came around on basketball, but only because it got her a full ride to college. Sylvia's grades still came home to Loretta, and if there was anything amiss, Sylvia knew she'd be hearing about it.)

By February 2005 Sylvia and Seimone were ranked No. 1 in the country. The duo finished with a pair of Final Fours, and Sylvia added another two for good measure, before the Chicago Sky selected her with the second pick in the 2008 WNBA Draft. (That girl from Naperville, Candace Parker, went just ahead of her, to the Los Angeles Sparks.)

Fowles was an instant star in Chicago, not to mention an immediate contributor for USA Basketball, but the Sky struggled to put a strong team around her. The one season they had regular-season success was 2013, Elena Delle Donne's rookie season, when they were beaten in the playoffs by the Fever, and then they followed a 15–19 regular season with a trip to the WNBA Finals in 2014 but were swept by the Mercury there.

So as Sylvia Fowles approached her eighth season, she wanted two things: comfort and her best chance to win. She also had soured on the Sky, where members of the front office had questioned her rehab process coming back from a hip injury. Dating back to ninth grade,

Fowles had instituted a system for herself to determine whether to trust someone or not: one strike, and it was over. Fowles recalled:

> [All the attention after I started dunking in ninth grade] did get a bit overwhelming. I think mostly because I'm low-key. I'd rather be treated like a human instead of some icon figure. I'm still that way today. I hate when people see me, and they'll be like, "Oh my gosh, Sylvia Fowles!" I'm like, "Look, I'm human too." . . . I'm so different from the basketball Sylvia in real life. Yeah, the name is what it is, and I think I took great strides to be where I'm at, but that [doesn't] define me. I don't feel like basketball defines who I am as a person. I just try to stay grounded in that area, but it definitely changed after that. People started treating me differently and making me seem like I was this special type of person, when in reality I'm just me.
>
> It's definitely hard to distinguish, especially at that age. You're in ninth grade—You don't know who is who. You think everybody is your friend in ninth grade . . . so it takes a lot of concentration to be like, "All right, start reading people for who they are." . . . I feel like if you've got good people [surrounding] you that it's easy to pick those people out really quick.

And this is where what Cheryl Reeve and Carley Knox had built really paid off. Other teams were gathering strength. The Los Angeles Sparks had finally figured out how to build around Candace Parker. New York was playing Bill Laimbeer ball with an attack centered around an in-prime Tina Charles. Mike Thibault, now in D.C., had the Mystics playing positionless basketball. And looming in college were the next two great WNBA stars, Breanna Stewart and A'ja Wilson, playing for UConn and South Carolina, respectively.

To keep that window open for as long as possible, the Lynx needed Sylvia Fowles too. And the team could point to more than just their other stars as a reason to come. The Lynx were cobranded with the Timberwolves everywhere, an unmistakable sign of equality. A brand-new practice facility opened in June 2015, just weeks before Sylvia officially arrived in Minnesota.

Pokey Chatman has been a shrewd negotiator throughout her time in the WNBA, but in this case she had no cards to play. She finally agreed to deal Fowles to the Lynx in late July as part of a three-team trade. The Lynx traded Damiris Dantas, Reshanda Gray, and a first-round pick to the Atlanta Dream. The Sky traded Fowles and a second-round pick to the Lynx. The Dream traded Erika de Souza—a versatile forward and former three-time All-Star but who was 33 years old and near the end of the line—to the Sky. That's all they had to show for the deal. "In my conversation with her, I think there were three reasons," Reeve said at the time of the deal for why Fowles had selected the Lynx. "Lindsay, Seimone, and Maya. People want to play with that group."

But there was also Seimone the person, who picked her up at the airport. They got food delivered to Seimone's place, and she sat Sylvia down and set about reassuring her before she'd even been in town for an hour. "Look, we brought you here to be you. We don't want you to do anything different. We just want you to play the way you're capable of playing," Sylvia remembered Seimone telling her. "Okay, in my mind, I'm like, 'Yeah, make sure Seimone gets her shots.'"

Fowles said this is the way the entire team treated her. Everyone understood the need to assimilate a new, vital player as a person, not just as an X on the whiteboard. She said:

> Mone too, she's a homebody. We could sit in the house for hours and just chitchat about any- and everything, and that's something that I love about her, 'cause we don't have to go out and do things to make our friendship closer-knitting. We just sit there and just talk about any- and everything. I remember Rebekkah asking me [if I needed] anything. Maya, Lindsay [were like], "What can I do to help you feel comfortable within our system?" I'm like, "Man, they're so giving of themselves. This is what I need to be. This is me. All of them [are] me."

That was almost a problem for Reeve and the Lynx—a champagne problem, one that any other team in the league would have happily signed up for, but a problem all the same. Minnesota was 12–4 at the time of the Fowles deal. But they proceeded to go 7–6 over the next month and were beaten 81–68 by the New York Liberty as August was coming to a close.

The Lynx were actually seventh in the league in net rating over that first month with Fowles, and despite a front court featuring the first- and fourth-most-prolific rebounders in the history of the league, the Lynx were seventh in rebounding percentage that first month as well.

An exasperated Cheryl Reeve met with us in the media at mid-court that night of the loss to the Liberty and bluntly telling us all that she and the Lynx were running out of time to figure it out. Reeve said:

We are different. A big part of our offense came through elbow actions. And my starting post players now—it's not really their forte. So we look a little different, and certain line-ups, we look a certain way, and we sub and look another way.

It's different, and four of my nine rotation players haven't been Lynx before. This is a bigger picture for us than people realize. There's years past—you can't help measuring us against past years. Luckily, our players realize our measuring stick is this season, against the other teams in the league right now.

That said, even Reeve was optimistic that night her team would figure it out. And part of that was an ongoing conversation with Sylvia, telling her she needed to assert herself. Fowles told me:

Me and Reeve had that conversation. She was like, "Syl, I want you to be you," and I'm like, "I am me. I am being me." She was like, "No, I want you to play the way you're capable of playing. I'm not telling you to be selfish." She's like, "Maya's gonna be Maya. Mone is gonna be Mone. She's gonna get her shots, and Lindsay's gonna be Lindsay, but I need you to play the way you're capable of playing." I think that's when everything just took off. I was like, "Okay, I am being nice, and I am being lovable, and godly, and giving of myself, but don't forget about self."

The Lynx finished the season at 22–12, good enough for the top seed in the Western Conference, and drew the Los Angeles Sparks, whose record of 14–20 didn't reflect their talent level. Candace Parker had missed half the season to spend some quality time with her family.

Nneka Ogwumike was blossoming into a star after getting selected first overall in the 2012 WNBA Draft, Kristi Toliver could hit a shot from anywhere, and Alana Beard was the best on-ball perimeter defender in the league.

But Moore found another level in Games 1 and 2, averaging 30 per game as the teams split, and 9,014 watched Minnesota overcome 28 and 13 from Parker to win Game 3 of the series 91–80 and advance. Moore, Whalen, Augustus, and Fowles all reached double figures, while Brunson played 39 minutes.

The Lynx would go on to beat the Taurasi-less Mercury in the Western Conference Finals, then exact revenge for 2012 on the Indiana Fever by winning a tight WNBA Finals in five games. Sylvia Fowles topped 20 points three times during the series and was named Finals MVP. And 18,933 fans saw her do it in Game 5. The crowd was a Lynx record, and it marked the first time Minnesota fans got to see the Lynx win a championship at home. It was another champagne problem—"My team keeps winning championships on the road"—but it was one the Lynx found a way to overcome, too.

A champagne-soaked Reeve said that night, sitting at the podium with the media after the win:

> I think Syl's been a great player for a long time. She's an Olympian for a reason. I think she was important to our team because she's so different than what we've had. So it's important that we acquire a player like that.
>
> Obviously, playing against Griner in the West, everybody's trying to get a little bit bigger. But I just think for us, being able to have that presence, it was going to take some pressure off great players like Lindsay, Seimone, and Maya.

I'm not sure we necessarily got more out of her. I think the series really suited her.

If you look at the strengths of our team, look at strengths of their team, we definitely targeted that one to five feet. It was a battle of one to five feet. You guys didn't talk about that very much. Indiana was persistent. They scored the second-highest points one to five feet, but they also gave up the second-worst percentage one to five feet. So we really viewed the series as a battle of one to five feet, and whoever won that in each game was who I thought was the victor in each game.

I think Sylvia Fowles coming here and embracing everything about what we do, being so coachable—when you're at the professional level, you don't see a player, when you call her name, that she looks at you in a way that she's eager to hear what you're about to say and even runs over to you. You don't see that in professional basketball. And so I think it's about—it's a testament to Syl. She had to hear some stuff that our team had a hard time incorporating her, that it was a problem having Sylvia Fowles.

I'd say the problem was the coach, you know, play-calling. Play-calling when she first got here, trying to figure her out and learn her. Syl just stayed with it no matter what. I'm so incredibly proud. I'm just so glad it worked out for her in this way.

The parade proceeded down a familiar route. Three championships in five years. A dynasty by any measure, this one punctuated with a private concert in Paisley Park from Prince. All three championship trophies rode in the last car, wielded by Moore and Augustus to the cheers of thousands.

And Reeve had made a promise to all of them—to Moore, Whalen, Augustus, Brunson, and Fowles. This would be the group for as long as they cared to stay. The Lynx would ride this car until the tank reached empty.

As Cheryl and Carley headed for their customary Hawaiian vacation to celebrate a championship, though, there were some big victories still to come before this team dispersed.

CHAPTER 8

CHANGE

———————

A S 2016 BEGAN, the garbage idea that only male coaches could lead WNBA teams to championships had been retired. Not only had Cheryl Reeve won three in five years from 2011 to 2015, in the two seasons she didn't—2012 and 2014—the teams that won were also helmed by women: Lin Dunn and Sandy Brondello, respectively. So it was no surprise that the Lynx re-signed Reeve to a long-term contract extension once again, keeping her in place for what would be the duration of the dynasty.

Reeve had become a figure of note throughout the state, an in-demand keynote speaker discussing everything from women's basketball itself to the impact of Title IX on the larger culture. Whalen, too, began adding speaking engagements, increasingly comfortable in those public forums. An understanding that something important was happening began to take hold in the larger culture. Reeve told Twin Cities Public Television in 2018:

Female athletes who get to see a woman in a leadership role—while you may not know it when you're 10 years old, or 14 years old, it starts to hit you more when you get a little bit older in life and you start to realize things that go on for women in the workplace, women in leadership roles. It's not until then that you look back and go, "Gosh, I didn't have any female role models. I didn't know what I could be." The ones that were, were so meaningful and powerful for me.

Just as no women's basketball players had to wonder whether high school basketball was for them once Peps Neuman came along, or consider an apex like the one Lindsay Whalen proved was possible, leading a WNBA team to the highest heights no longer lived in the realm of the hypothetical as Reeve's run with the Lynx, and their success, extended year after year. And as the Lynx prepared for the 2016 season, one in which they'd have the kind of depth to match their star power in the starting lineup, the eyes of the women's basketball world once again turned to a superstar operating out of the Twin Cities: Rachel Banham.

The Year of Banham actually started back in 2015, when she completed her rehab from her torn ACL and partially torn MCL and got back onto the court. By the fall, she knew her Gophers would have to win with additional scoring on the outside, now that Amanda Zahui B. had made the leap to the WNBA—getting selected second overall in the 2015 draft—as had Shae Kelley, a forward who the Lynx drafted in the third round and who played eight games with them in 2015. That duo represented 48 percent of the team's points and, more critically, 50 percent of their rebounds.

The Gophers had made 214 threes in 2014–15. It was a program record. They'd need more shots from deep to get back to the NCAA tournament and overcome their lack of experienced size. Banham did what she could, and that turned out to be *a lot*. The records started falling early in the season. Banham had an unfair advantage over Whalen when it came to setting the all-time scoring record at Minnesota, thanks to that 10-game fourth season and redshirt additional year. Whalen played in 113 games total, while Banham beat her scoring mark in game 117. Sadly, the moment wasn't experienced by the home fans at Williams Arena, the way Banham had always pictured it happening, but rather by a crowd of just 110 at a Thanksgiving weekend tournament in San Juan, Puerto Rico. Unfortunately, the game typified what so often happened to the Banham-era Gophers, who did not have enough help around her. Banham scored 29, and Minnesota lost in OT.

Banham returned home and was properly celebrated at Williams Arena on December 12, 2015, scoring 23 and helping Minnesota beat Memphis 70–60. Lindsay was there too, calling Banham a worthy holder of the record. People threw around the idea of Banham scoring 3,000 points in her career, but such a mark would require the kind of season that no one had ever had at Minnesota, and few had accomplished anywhere.

No one could figure out how to slow her down in the 2015–16 season. She scored 17 against North Dakota on December 23, 2015, and 17 against Rutgers on December 31, 2015. These stand out because they were the only two games all season in which she didn't score 20 or more—no one held her below 20 at all once the calendar turned to 2016. The consistency was just mind-boggling.

She scored 30 or more 10 times. But she wasn't doing it by using too many possessions. She finished north of 50 percent from two, and at 39 percent from three, even as she expanded to an average 9.5 attempts from beyond the arc. Her assist percentage was 24.3 percent, so she never stopped getting her teammates involved, and her turnover percentage was just 11.5 percent, which reflects Banham splitting a lot of double teams. Her steal percentage of 3 percent means she simply didn't take plays off.

And she saved some of her biggest performances for the road, and even heard about it from some fans. "It was so hilarious," Banham remembered. "I had people coming up to me, being like, 'You need to score this much in the Barn, and we want to see it.' I was like, 'Ugh, I'm *trying*.' And I was having, like, 30-point games. You know, I was averaging dang near 30."

She finished the 2015–16 season at 28.6 points per game, and her transcendent performances, at home and away, drew national attention. There was the night she scored 60 at Northwestern on February 7, 2016. The Gophers won in two overtimes, 112–106. Banham had nine rebounds in that one, plus four assists and two steals. She did it on just 32 shots. It tied an NCAA all-time scoring record. But only 1,223 people were on hand to see it.

There are a couple of lessons from Banham's senior season. One is that the game had truly become national. Banham couldn't score 60 in isolation. It was national news, even with the game taking place in front of a sparse road crowd. Banham remembered the moment two days after she scored 60, when Kobe Bryant tweeted at her about it. "I was literally shaking," Banham told *USA Today*. "I felt like I was going to start crying. I was so happy." She ran around the Bierman

Building, through the women's basketball offices and practice facility, showing the tweet to everyone. She tried to play it cool online rather than tweeting back right away and "say[ing] something dumb and . . . embarrassing."

And then she kept on scoring. By the time the postseason rolled around, though, Banham's Gophers were on the outside looking in for the NCAA tournament. Banham scored like no one had in program history, but the team simply didn't have enough defending to make it stand up, and the Gophers headed to the Women's National Invitation Tournament (WNIT).

Finally, the Williams Arena fans got to experience a historic night with Banham on March 16, 2016, when she scored 48 points in an 87–80 victory over Milwaukee. That was more points than anyone had ever scored, men or women, in a college game at Williams Arena. It was a WNIT record. It also pushed Banham past the following people on the all-time NCAA scoring list: Cheryl Miller, Maya Moore, and Elena Delle Donne. "Really proud of Rachel, obviously," her head coach, Marlene Stollings, said that night. "She continues to annihilate records. [We are] witnessing history every time she steps on the floor." To this day, Vicky Nelson and Peps Neuman say it is the single greatest performance they've ever witnessed live.

"All these records don't really hit me now, but down the road I will really appreciate it," Banham said that night. "It's crazy when you hear those names, because they are players I looked up to, so right now it's really weird. It hasn't really hit me, but I know I'll appreciate it a lot more."

The final tally: 3,093 points. And yet only 1,663 people were there to see her score 48, and only 3,224 watched the final game in Rachel

Banham's Minnesota career, a 37-point explosion in a WNIT loss to South Dakota.

This is where it's important to define what Rachel Banham meant, and didn't mean, to Minnesota, and vice versa. It was never going to be fair to ask Rachel Banham, by herself, to "save" the Minnesota program. It wasn't a program that needed saving. It was a program that needed a coaching staff that recruited well both in and outside of Minnesota, aided by an administration that invested in the program at a level at or above what their competitors in the Big Ten and nationally were spending. Lindsay Whalen's years as a player don't serve as some example that every team that follows should have to live up to by themselves. Whalen's Gophers career represents the kind of promise available to the University of Minnesota, should it choose to go all in on women's basketball, like we see elsewhere in the Big Ten.

But the program's existence also allowed Banham to stay home, have an epic collegiate career, and position herself to play professionally. No longer was it necessary to create her own team or barnstorm to have that kind of experience. "I knew I was blowing up on the scene more, that my stock was going up," Banham told me. "And that was cool. But I wasn't even thinking about it. I knew it was going to handle itself. I was playing a high level of basketball, and it was going to work out."

No longer was the question asked, as the WNBA Draft arrived, whether Banham should stick around to "save the Lynx." Whether there'd be a league for her to play in was no longer a question, either.

Women's basketball was a place to ply her trade. How successful college and pro teams were had to do with how effectively they utilized their skills on the sporting and business sides of the ledger, no different than the measurements of men's sports for the past century. The gaps remained. But the myths of how to close those gaps continued to evaporate, not only for observers of the game but for those in the game themselves.

Banham's April wasn't anything like the immediate post-college experiences of the generations before her. There was no hard stop—there was winning the three-point contest at the NCAA Men's Final Four, then flying to Los Angeles, where she'd been nominated for the John R. Wooden Award as best college player (and finally got to meet Kobe Bryant). Then it was jet-setting across the country to Connecticut, where the 2016 WNBA Draft would take place at Mohegan Sun Arena.

Banham was ready to go wherever she was selected, and there would be no objections around Minnesota when the Connecticut Sun snared another favorite daughter of the North Star State, once again fourth overall in the 2016 draft, just behind the trio of UConn Huskies from their incredible 2016 team—Breanna Stewart, Moriah Jefferson, and Morgan Tuck. The Lynx traded their 14th overall pick for the veteran guard Jia Perkins, who joined with Renee Montgomery to form a bench backcourt as potent as many starting units around the league, while dealing Devereaux Peters for Natasha Howard, a preternaturally gifted defender whose emerging offensive game made her as dangerous a two-way force off the bench as anyone in the WNBA. No one minded that the Lynx and Rachel Banham were each striking out on their own. The world of women's basketball was big enough for all of it.

By late April, the world learned that 4 of the 12 2016 USA Basketball women's players were from the Minnesota Lynx: Moore, Augustus,

Whalen, and Fowles. No other team had as large a contingent. The assistant coach, once again, was Reeve. "The fact that you've got four players on the team from the Minnesota Lynx is not a coincidence," head coach Geno Auriemma told the *Star Tribune* at the time. "You're talking about four of the very best players in the world, and four incredibly unselfish individuals. The fact that those four spend time together, practice together, know each other—that goes a long way."

The Lynx knew precisely who they were from the start, and bested their own previous WNBA record for wins to start a season. They'd begun 2012 10–0 but ran their record to 13–0 in 2016 with a victory over the Los Angeles Sparks on June 21, 2016, before L.A. finally ended their unbeaten streak in a rematch at Target Center on June 24, 2016, in front of 13,003 fans energized by the growing rivalry, a precursor to the playoff battles ahead.

But just a couple weeks later, the on-court drama took a back seat to more important matters. On the night of July 6, 2016, Philando Castile, a 32-year-old Black man, was driving with his girlfriend, Diamond Reynolds. The two of them were pulled in Falcoln Heights, MN, less than 20 minutes from the Target Center. Officer Jeronimo Yanez asked for Castile's license and registration, at which point Castile informed Yanez that he had a firearm, which he was licensed to carry. Yanez told him not to take it out, and Castile informed him he wouldn't. And he didn't. And it didn't matter. Yanez then shot him 7 times anyway, and 20 minutes later, Castile was dead.

Reynolds had the presence of mind to put the incident on Facebook Live, shining a light on this horrific encounter. There are countless stories like this, but the sheer volume of them seemed to blend them together in the public consciousness. This hit different.

Protests sprang up all over the country. And the moment, coming just a day after Alton Sterling was shot and killed by Baton Rouge police officers (another episode of police violence captured on video and distributed via social media around the world) and a day before Micah Xavier Johnson targeted, shot, and killed five Dallas police officers, left so many feeling angry, sad, and determined not to let this moment pass without making an effort to change this trajectory.

The Minnesota Lynx, in particular, felt the moment had come to utilize their platform once again. With one victim in Seimone Augustus's hometown and another just a few miles from the Lynx's home, this felt personal to them. So prior to Minnesota's July 9, 2016, game against the Dallas Wings, the four Lynx captains—Brunson, Whalen, Moore, and Augustus—held a press conference. Each one wore a shirt with a simple message on the front: CHANGE STARTS WITH US—JUSTICE & ACCOUNTABILITY. On the back was a Black Lives Matter logo and a Dallas PD logo. "If we take this time to see that this is a human issue and speak out together, we can greatly decrease fear and create change," Moore said that night. "Tonight we will be wearing shirts to honor and mourn the losses of precious American citizens and to plead for change in all of us." Then the Lynx went out and beat the Wings, formerly the Tulsa Shock (and formerly the Detroit Shock), 93–56.

To understand how significant this moment was, one need look no further than the immediate backlash to it. Four off-duty Minneapolis police officers, despite the full spectrum of the player message, walked off the job as security guards at the Lynx game (while the head of their police union took a shot at WNBA crowd sizes, saying only four officers were on the job because "the Lynx have such a pathetic draw").

Other WNBA players also protested in support of the message, with the New York Liberty following suit the next day. Eventually they were joined by the Indiana Fever and Phoenix Mercury. Notable too was Tina Charles, then of the Liberty, who wore her warm-up shirt inside out while receiving Player of the Month honors from the league on July 21. The WNBA's response was to fine all teams who continued to wear plain black T-shirts instead of their league-mandated shirts during pregame warm-ups.

The anger reached a boiling point following that July 21 game. The media was told ahead of the postgame that players would only speak about police violence and their efforts to protest it. We entered the New York Liberty locker room, and veteran Tanisha Wright, Tina Charles, and now-Liberty forward Swin Cash spoke about the past few weeks. "If they're trying to silence us on our platform wearing our T-shirts, then we can use [the media] as a platform and just use you guys to try to force this matter," Charles told us.

And Swin added: "We would just hope the league would be more open to working with the players. Because like Tanisha said, the majority of our players are passionate about this. The majority of our players care about this. The majority of our players are affected by this. And it's something that has to change."

The collective support resounded around the league. Cash responded to the police union's snark, saying:

> Here's a team that has brought a number of championships to put Minnesota on the map, and so to have women that have played at the highest level . . . basically to insult not only them but their fans—which Minnesota has an unbelievable

fan base there—that probably said more about [the police] than the Lynx players. Also I think [the union head], by making those comments, that's exactly why the players are asking for more dialogue and to have more conversations.

That it was collective action was enormously important as well, as Tamika Catchings made clear to us when we walked into the Indiana Fever locker room. "Players are branching out, and the players are really taking ahold of this," she said that day at Madison Square Garden.

As a source familiar with the league's thinking at the time put it to me, "We understood pretty quickly that continuing to fine the players was not a road we could travel down."

More than a month later, 49ers quarterback Colin Kaepernick kneeled, rather than stood, for the national anthem ahead of an NFL game. Megan Rapinoe did the same ahead of a U.S. Women's National Soccer Team game the following week. All of it followed the Minnesota Lynx's actions.

Within days, the WNBA rescinded the fines. But it went further than that. The WNBA understood in that moment, and has been animated by this understanding since, that there is no neutral ground when it comes to social justice. The WNBA, an entity that for years lived in fear of frightening away "families"—the shorthand for cisgender, heteronormative families—and had silenced its appeal to the LGBTQ+ community would instead marry the great game of women's basketball itself to the social progress its growth helped facilitate.

Put another way: it started doing things the Minnesota Lynx way. Everything that followed descended from the Lynx, from the Seattle

Storm publicly aligning with Planned Parenthood; to Natasha Cloud of the Washington Mystics working publicly with Moms Demand Action for years to work to prevent gun violence; to the entire league dedicating the 2020 season to justice for Breonna Taylor, another Black woman killed by senseless police violence; to the Atlanta Dream itself rebelling against a white supremacist owner, Kelly Loeffler, and not only organizing on behalf of Loeffler's opponent in the 2020 U.S. Senate race that tipped the balance of power to the Democrats but also forcing her to sell the team to a group that included Renee Montgomery. Renee had played for the Atlanta Dream. Prior to that? She was part of the 2016 Minnesota Lynx.

When I asked Montgomery via email whether the actions of the Lynx in early July 2016 made all that followed within the league possible, she responded:

> I think that's definitely a fair characterization. Because the amount of pushback we got from fans and the league was because sports had never seen anything like that before. It was always separate, and that year it collided, just like in 2020. I remember Tina getting fined in New York, them wearing black shirts or turning their shirts inside out. Our ownership and leadership groups for the Lynx fully supported our protest, so it made us confident to continue. That year was a struggle to say the least, but I do feel it jump-started what we see today with message pieces on shirts and helmets.

In the process, it did two other things as well. It helped the centerpiece of those Lynx teams, Maya Moore, find her passion for work outside of basketball for the first time in her life. And in that way, it led to the end of the Lynx as they existed for much of the decade. After the 2016 season, Moore decided to stay home instead of playing overseas. It enabled her body to rest, yes, but it also allowed her mind to roam in vital new directions. Moore wrote:

> It was a blessing to begin to unlock this side of me that I hadn't been able to really develop because of my commitment to the grind. . . . I poured myself into learning what it meant for me to be a citizen. I had been an athlete all my life, but I was also a citizen. I began to have extensive conversations with lawyers and watch documentaries and read books and really pay more attention so I could learn. There was so much I had to understand and discover.

After changing the paradigm for the way athletes related their public and political selves to the public, the Lynx had a WNBA title to chase, once their contingent returned from the Olympics with another gold medal.

By the playoffs, it was obvious the class of the league could be found in Minnesota and Los Angeles. The Lynx finished 28–6, Reeve winning her second WNBA Coach of the Year honors and Fowles her third Defensive Player of the Year honors (first with the Lynx). But the Sparks were right on their tail at 26–8. Nneka Ogwumike completed the most efficient shooting season in WNBA history, with a true shooting percentage of 73.7 percent, and won league MVP honors. Candace Parker dominated alongside her in the front court, while Kristi Toliver made 42.4 percent of her threes and nobody got past Alana Beard at the defensive end.

Better yet, the league changed its playoff format and did away with conferences, so the two would not meet up until the WNBA Finals, assuming each managed to get through its semifinal tests—and each did, the Lynx sweeping the Phoenix Mercury despite Diana Taurasi's return to the league, and the Sparks beating the Chicago Sky in four games.

What followed was the best WNBA Finals anyone could ever remember. Think of it this way: The WNBA honored its 20 greatest players ever at the half of Game 1 of the Finals to commemorate the league's 20th anniversary. Four of the 20—Parker for Los Angeles and Moore, Augustus, and Whalen for Minnesota—were playing in the game. Reeve said prior to the series that it would likely be decided by "minutiae"—free throws or an out-of-bounds play. Or, well, officiating.

The Sparks won Game 1 in Minnesota 78–76 after the Lynx managed to deny the ball to Candace Parker and Chelsea Gray, the two players Coach Brian Agler's last-second play was designed for, and Alana Beard was forced to take a 21-footer at the buzzer, and made it. She had never made a game-winning shot at any level, Beard told assembled reporters after the game.

Before Game 2, Reeve had to answer questions about the way her team would adjust to stop Los Angeles's pick-and-roll game, and also, of course, how presidential candidate Donald Trump had gabbed about his ability to grab women "by the pussy." Reeve did not shy away from the moment. "Donald Trump's candidacy has shined a light on so many problems that exist that I always talk about," Reeve told reporters during a media availability on October 12, 2016. "He is the epitome of all these things. He is not alone. It is behavior that's been accepted for years."

While the nation (well, some of the nation) recoiled from Trump's remarks, the Lynx went out and evened the series in a 79–60 victory behind 21 points and 12 rebounds from Maya Moore to send it back to Los Angeles for Game 3 tied 1–1.

The Sparks won Game 3, though, 92–75, and the Lynx faced elimination on the road in Game 4. The Lynx rode a familiar path to victory, though—31 points for Maya Moore, and a 41–25 edge on the glass—and all that stood between the Lynx and a fourth championship in six years was a win at home in front of the Target Center crowd. The crowd of 19,423 people who packed Target Center broke another record. The Sparks, though, were not cowed, with clutch god Chelsea Gray scoring 11 points during one stretch, and a Candace Parker shot put the Sparks ahead 71–63 with 3:06 left.

Minnesota roared back, however, and a Whalen steal, followed by her racing down the floor for a breakaway layup, tied the game at 71. The crowd erupted; 19,423 people never sounded so loud.

The Lynx proceeded to utterly lock up the Sparks, forcing Nneka Ogwumike to take a shot after the shot clock reached zero. But officials did not stop the action to review the shot, then used the fact that the game had continued as a reason to declare they *couldn't* review the shot. An official had even signaled for a review at the time. After that, greats rose to the occasion. It just so happened that after Parker and Moore traded hoops, Ogwumike got the last one, with two seconds left. The Sparks were champions.

It was understandably hard for Reeve to let it go. She said at the time:

A couple things I want to do first. First is to congratulate the L.A. Sparks for a great series, hard-fought. They deserved winning. They did some things today that were necessary to put them over the top.

The second thing is I want to—as I expressed to these guys, this is a really special group led by Seimone, Maya. We had a great season that didn't end the way we wanted it to, but I'm no less proud today than on the days that we actually won a championship.

And then I want to do like other teams do, which is bemoan the officiating in that they botched a call at 1:14. Nneka Ogwumike's shot was not good. It was reviewable at the time when she shot it. The referees at that point didn't think anything was wrong. They didn't understand it was the end of the clock. They didn't hear the shot clock.

When they put the ball in play, the play is no longer reviewable, yet in the first quarter, three or four minutes or five minutes can go by until the next stoppage of play before a review. So it's really unfortunate that players continually put themselves out there playing and competing at a really high level, whether it was the eight-second call in the game in L.A.—doesn't matter, okay? The game today, it's not fair to the players. It's not enough just to apologize and send out a memo that they got something wrong, okay? These players are so invested, and something must be done about the officiating in this league because it is not fair to these great players that we have.

Even so, Reeve was already thinking ahead to 2017 in that post-game press conference. "I don't know; they just said 'Stick a fork in it' last year, and all we did was get back to the Finals and have the best record in the league," she said. "I don't know, maybe you guys should start writing how we're old and washed-up, and maybe it motivates them."

Ultimately, though everyone conceded the Lynx were right on the merits, and the league chose not to replay the final 1:14 of its championship. It's impossible to say the Lynx would have prevailed if the call had been reversed in real time, or if that final 1:14 had been played a second time. But it's hard, to this day, for the Lynx not to wonder what would have happened.

How hard? Well, when I asked Carley Knox how she and Cheryl handled what happened in the fall of 2016, her response with a laugh was, "Yeah. Lots of things happened in 2016. I don't know if you're talking about the election or on the court." I specified that I was referring to the election of Donald Trump but allowed that I understood she could have thought I meant the final minute-plus of the WNBA Finals. Knox replied:

> Let's just say it was a rough year overall. I just couldn't believe it. I am the eternal optimist. Cheryl tends to be— she calls herself a realist. I like to tease her and call her the negativist. We have a nice yin and yang going. I kept saying, "It's not going to happen. It's not going to happen. Hillary's going to win. There's no way. There's no way."
>
> I just member sitting there watching the TV into the wee hours of the night. I'm like, "There's no way. There's no way." Finally I went to bed and I woke up and started crying because it was so devastating. How you can think that there's that much ignorance and hate in the world. Especially after all the progress we had made in the preceding years

where you're like, "Oh, hey, we're really getting somewhere."
Then just seeing the platform that he ran on and some of the
hate and ignorance that was perpetuated and those people
coming out of the woodwork and feeling empowered to be
hateful.

Just months earlier, Carley had joined Cheryl at yet another meeting at the White House. President Obama had noticed that Oliver was
upset—Cheryl was up on stage but he wasn't. So Cheryl went into the
crowd, brought Ollie over, and said, "Say 'Hi, Mr. President'"—and
Ollie high-fived Barack Obama.

Now it would be a new and different fight. But it was one Knox
was ready for. She said:

> It was devastating, but you had to get up and keep going. It
> was a new day and [we had to] keep fighting the fight every
> single day and do what we [could] to make our little imprint
> on the world and keep fighting so that our son has a better
> world in which to live, and I hope that one day he'll be a
> part of change in the world, and in his little way I think he
> already is by being so loving and so kind and so sensitive.
>
> You've just got to keep fighting. Just like the WNBA.
> We lost our team in Detroit, but I didn't give up on the
> league. I wanted to keep fighting to make sure we never lost
> another WNBA team.

CHAPTER 9

HOME

———

THE NEXT YEAR, 2017, began with Rachel Banham's No. 1 being raised into the Williams Arena rafters. Her number and picture reside on a banner right next to the picture and No. 13 of her idol, Lindsay Whalen.

The New Year's Day celebration swelled the crowd to 4,884, with hundreds lining up to get Banham's autograph. The Gophers lost, though, 83–72 to Maryland, with a former coach—Brenda Oldfield, now Brenda Frese—still at the helm of the No. 4 team in the country. Meanwhile, Minnesota's coach, Marlene Stollings, would bolt after the 2017–18 season, leaving Minnesota for Texas Tech and a massive pay raise. The Gophers found a replacement, and managed to pay her less than Stollings's $500,000: Lindsay Whalen. (Frese, like Iowa coach Lisa Bluder, now makes north of $1 million per season.)

Meanwhile, the 2017 Lynx had one more championship run in them, but already Maya Moore felt as if life was taking her in another direction. She'd become more and more invested in the effort to free a convict named Jonathan Irons from prison. (Irons, who is Black, was wrongfully convicted of the burglary and shooting of a white homeowner outside of St. Louis in 1998.) And suddenly, a woman who never stopped thinking about basketball—I still remember interviewing her during the off-season courtside at a high school All-American game, and even as we spoke she saw a basketball and grabbed it, began idly dribbling, even in a skirt and heels—couldn't focus on it in the same way. Moore wrote:

> As I had discovered more of myself, more of my purpose, and what my heart beats for, the more I felt the urge to live in that purpose. So shifting back to an in-season lifestyle was pretty jarring for my soul. As the 2017 WNBA season began, I found out my heart was not in it the way I was used to. I just didn't have it. My passion was at an all-time low, and I wasn't sure how to process it.
>
> Yes, I would call this my passionless season, but I still played hard and (spoiler alert) the Lynx still won the WNBA championship.
>
> It was the weirdest and most unnatural thing to feel this way. Anybody who knows me knows that I'm all in with whatever I do with passion and determination. Yes, I've probably said that before, but I'm mentioning it again because this was so unlike me to feel this way. I'm the conviction person, but it seemed like my convictions were living somewhere other than Basketballville.

We should all be so successful when we're passionless—Moore averaged 17.3 points per game, hit 41.1 percent of her threes, and made yet another All-Star team. Fowles led the team in scoring at

18.9 per contest, fully remembering not to forget about self amid her life of selflessness and winning league MVP honors in the process.

The Lynx led the league in offensive efficiency and defensive efficiency. And their net rating of +14.2 not only led the league, it was the best mark the Lynx had put up in any of their seasons. The 2017 Lynx heavily resembled the 2016 Lynx, though age and injuries began slowing Whalen down, who was largely in a point guard timeshare with Montgomery, and Plenette Pierson of the Detroit Shock was brought in to play the part of Taj McWilliams-Franklin, the sage older center, to back up Sylvia Fowles.

The Target Center was undergoing renovations, so the Lynx were moved to the Xcel Energy Center in St. Paul for the regular season. Then during the postseason, the Minnesota Wild of the NHL (Championships? Zero.) took precedence over the Lynx, so they got moved again. Their postseason home? Williams Arena. No busted pipe necessary.

It was another classic series between the 27–7 Lynx and 26–8 Sparks, once again clearly the class of the WNBA. "We assumed it was going to be us two again, with the way they've been playing and the way we've been playing," Seimone Augustus said prior to Game 1 to the Associated Press. "It was almost inevitable, like it was going to happen."

Or as the *Star Tribune* scribe Kent Youngblood put it as the series began: "Everything to this point, it seems, has been superfluous."

Game 1 was three games in itself—Los Angeles began the game on a 28–2 run, the Lynx climbed all the way back, and then Chelsea Gray hit a buzzer-beater to make the entire comeback moot.

The Lynx returned fire with a 70–68 win in Game 2, the 5 start-ers scoring 63 of their 70 points, all 5 tallying between 11 and 14, as balanced as possible.

The Sparks won Game 3 75–64, setting up another chance for Los Angeles to clinch at home in Game 4. The Lynx once again spoiled that plan, 80–69; Sylvia Fowles was impossible to stop, with 22 points and 14 rebounds. The Lynx outrebounded the Sparks 48–28. The central plank in Cheryl Reeve's plan remained a critical part of the team's identity. And Fowles was the reason the window stayed open as long as it did.

Back to Game 5 at the Barn, and 14,632 packed the grand old arena. Vicky and Peps, of course, were there. Lynx and Timberwolves owner Glen Taylor was there too. His Timberwolves were playing a game in China. "But I wasn't going to miss this," Taylor said, happily enjoying the festivities at Williams Arena. After the game, Glen and his wife, Becky, got a photo with Peps.

Karen Healey Lange and Kim Franchi were there too. They weren't sitting in their original seats, which had been right behind Carley's mom—too rowdy for her, they were moved.

Franchi told me:

> We were at a playoff game. And we were sitting on the end of the court, off to the side a little bit. And there was a security guard right next to us. And they were playing the Sparks, and I'm standing up screaming, "Refs, you suck! Nneka, you're flopping!" on the floor and Carley's running up to us, and she's like, "This is how you guys behave at a game?" The security guy was looking at us, and I'm like, "Why, are we gonna get thrown out? We're

not cursing or anything. Are we gonna get thrown out of here?"

And I'm like, "This is what you do at games, especially when it's a playoff game." It's like giving blood out there on the court.

Carley moved her mom so she could watch the game in peace, and Kim and Karen could cheer Philly-style.

So Cheryl's past was definitely present. So too were some of the next generation of women's basketball greats. Paige Bueckers, now a star at UConn, grew up going to Lynx games while becoming the first Minnesota player to win Gatorade Player of the Year as a sophomore. She remembers being star-struck as a fifth grader, working on her shot at a local gym, when a woman approached her with some tips on how to get better: Cheryl Reeve. A few years later, Reeve realized she had been talking to *the* Paige Bueckers, but Bueckers could barely speak, very aware in that moment she was talking to *the* Cheryl Reeve.

"She's a generational talent," Reeve told Minnesota Public Radio in 2021. "You can spot those at a very young age. I was really glad to see that it was a young girl, and I needed to acknowledge that. I didn't know what it was going to turn into, but I was happy she was there hooping, and I wanted to let her know that."

Minnesota, incidentally, came in second for her collegiate services, and many around the program believe that if the Gophers had hired Lindsay Whalen just a little sooner, Bueckers would have stayed home and played home games at the Barn. At the time of this writing, fans all over Minnesota are trying to figure out how the Lynx can bring Paige Bueckers home. "They were amazing to watch, and they were part of the reason why I fell in love with the game," Bueckers told Jim Souhan of the *Star Tribune* in June 2023. "Just to be able to watch Maya, Lindsay, Rebekkah, Sylvia, that whole core, and all of the role players was amazing. Especially in the Barn, where everything was so animated and the fans were super into it."

Mara Braun was there too. She was a 6'0" guard entering her sophomore season as this book was written, an elite two-way player who did stay home for school, recruited by Whalen, part of an incredible class of four Minnesota stars—Braun, forward Nia Holloway, forward Mallory Heyer, and guard Amaya Battle. Braun told me in November 2022:

> It was cool to be able to see that place sold out and know that it's possible, and it's possible for a women's game to do that. And obviously, watching Coach Whalen and knowing how much of an impact she has on the community and the people in Minnesota—she's winning, and people want to go watch her. . . . And so I feel like it was just kind of like a moment for us to say, "Okay, this can happen and we've just got to work for it." Because, I mean, she tells us all the time, it didn't come easy. It took a long time. There were a lot of lumps in there. But eventually they got to be this super, amazing team.

Another big recruit the Lynx brought to women's basketball? Caitlin Clark, who grew up a huge Maya Moore fan, the Lynx the closest WNBA team to her in Des Moines. And she experienced equal parts of the team Cheryl Reeve created and the business operations Carley Knox fostered. She said:

Yeah, absolutely. It's actually kind of a crazy story. I've loved the Lynx, and I forget what happened, but my dad . . . was like, "All right, I'll take you to the Lynx game." So I was like, "All right, let's go."

So we're road-tripping to Minneapolis, and we're in the hotel, and I think I went swimming before . . . with my dad in the hotel pool. He called the ticket office: "Oh, I want to bring my daughter to the game." The guy at the ticket office—no clue who he is or where he is now—he's like, "Oh, do you guys want to come before the game and sit on the court and see all this stuff?"

My dad was like, "Oh, absolutely, she would love that." He got me like a Rebekkah Brunson shirt, and Lindsay Whalen came over, Seimone Augustus came over. Clearly, I don't even know how old I was, but these are vivid memories in my mind, and they were playing the Seattle Storm.

So I think it was just—I think that just shows how much I loved the game from a very young age, and at the same time, that inspired me even more. When I got to go and experience something like that, but also the arena was packed for the Lynx. They love the Lynx, but because the Lynx were really, really good. They had dominance there for quite some time.

And Lindsay Whalen is one of the best point guards ever to touch a basketball. So I grew up really inspired by that team, and I think, you know, when I was able to go to a game, that only encouraged that more.

The Lynx did not disappoint that crowd, winning their fourth title in seven years, 85–76. Moore had 18 points, Fowles and Whalen each added 17, Augustus 14, Brunson 13. The entire Sparks team had 29 rebounds. The Lynx grabbed 46, and Sylvia had 20 of them herself, breaking her own Finals record of 17—set the week before, earlier in the series—en route to a second WNBA Finals MVP award.

That night when it was all over—four titles in seven years—Reeve told assembled media:

> I can't tell you how blessed I feel to just be around these guys every day. You know, most importantly about this group, we let each other be ourselves, and there is so much to be said for that. I'm not easy to be around, and our staff—I think about our daily process together, and like I said, you guys aren't in it every day, so you don't know. Obviously it's the most special time in our lives from a professional standpoint, but it's the people. It's the people that we do it with that just—we're in it for life, this group. We're in it for life, and that's just an incredible blessing that I feel to be able to be around it every single day.

The Lynx as we knew them broke up after one more season, 2018, Cheryl riding them until the tank hit empty, as she promised. Maya played through 2018 and then stepped away from the game, never to return. She threw herself into freeing Jonathan Irons, and won, as Maya almost always does. She and Irons wed in 2020, nine days after his release from prison, and she is now the mother to Jonathan Jr., born February 7, 2022. There is an argument to be made that Maya Moore is the greatest player in the history of the WNBA. And if she falls short because her career didn't last long enough, because she instead chose to work to free an innocent man from prison, she'd be just fine with that too.

Lindsay also played through 2018, the same year the University of Minnesota hired her to be their women's basketball coach. About Whalen, Reeve told Sloane Martin back in 2018:

> I recognize her impact maybe more than her. To be able to know that you've touched that many lives, it's not something, while you're in it, that you can fully grasp. It's going to be many, many years from now that Lindsay's going to look back and maybe understand what all of us have said about her.
>
> I bet she could run for governor and be successful. She could do anything. To be a state's favorite daughter is just like—to be one of the all-time greatest sports figures in the history of a state—she transcends the male-female thing. . . . Lindsay, bar none, male or female, is one of the best basketball players ever.

Seimone played with the Lynx through 2019, then signed with the rival Sparks for 2020. Ultimately, though, she returned to Minnesota to have her number retired in 2022. And down in Baton Rouge? They made her into a statue at LSU. "I didn't do this alone," Seimone, crying, told the crowd gathered at the statue unveiling in January 2023, her mom and dad in the crowd. "A lot of the female athletes here from my time were an inspiration. We were all going on our own race, our own journey, and I do stand here proudly as a representation of all those women. So many great female athletes have come through LSU that have made statements in their respective sports. I won't be the last one that will be acknowledged."

Rebekkah Brunson's No. 32 also will never be worn by another member of the Minnesota Lynx; it was retired in 2022. While finding a home in the dispersal draft isn't easy, Rebekkah has in Minnesota, where she's served as both an assistant to Reeve and as an analyst on Timberwolves broadcasts. "She was so much a part of our will," Reeve told Minnpost.com back in 2022. "Her determination to defend the team's best post player, finish plays with rebounds, get us extra possessions on the glass . . . she would put herself physically out there in ways you could always count on. Shootaround, game, didn't matter when it was. She had that will. It was internal. It was innate to her. That's why every team she was on had success."

And Sylvia? Her No. 34 was retired in 2023. She was the last Lynx dynasty member to leave the court. She finished her career second in WNBA history in win shares, with 73.5; only Tamika Catchings ahead of her. Fowles is the best center in WNBA history, and anybody who says otherwise is wrong.

EPILOGUE:
PEPS'S PLACE

T'S COLD IN early November in Minnesota but nice and warm inside Williams Arena, where Peps Neuman and Vicky Nelson—wearing matching gold Minnesota Golden Gophers hoodies and maroon pants, and seated in their customary first-row perch courtside—are taking in their first live look at four freshmen who are expected to define the University of Minnesota program for years to come, in a nonconference game against Western Illinois.

Peps is drawn to Amaya Battle, the playmaking point guard who came of age alongside Paige Bueckers at Hopkins, while Nelson is impressed by Braun, the two-way shooting guard who posted the best freshman season of the group. They all live together, they all share a common goal: to restore Minnesota to its former glory, and maybe, since Whalen came up two wins shy of a title, even exceed it.

"We love it here," Peps said, eager to show me around. "This is like home."

Peps turned 78 in October 2022, but her energy level is seemingly unchanged. "Have you ever seen the top of this place? You gotta come check it out," she said to me, and at halftime, she bounded up the stairs of the Barn as I worked to keep pace with her.

She looked down on the arena's vast bowl as we reached the top. "Isn't it beautiful?" she said. It is.

There was plenty to like that night for Lindsay Whalen, asked to build the program on the strength of her name and history but forced to do so into the teeth not only of COVID but a Big Ten engaged in an arms race the University of Minnesota wasn't always prepared to win. Her salary also checked in around a quarter of Ben Johnson's, the men's coach, who signed a five-year, $9.75 million contract in March 2021.

Still, on this night, it was possible to dream of the Barn being full again. What Peps and Cheryl and Carley and Lindsay have wrought is a state that ranks atop the United States in women's basketball for per capita participation, according to analysis by the *Star Tribune*. Across sports, girls' participation runs equal to or slightly ahead of the boys from 2012 to 2022 in Minnesota. The promise of Title IX is so often belied by the reality. Here, in this measurement, Minnesota has found equality.

Young women across Minnesota—a gymnast who proved too tall and switched to basketball, such as Mallory Heyer; a little sister who played with her brother and held her own, such as Braun; a multisport athlete and activist such as Nia Holloway, who founded the Black Student Union at Eden Prairie High School; a big-picture thinker such as Amaya Battle, who can simultaneously appreciate how far women's basketball has come and how much more progress remains elusive.

Battle told me in November 2022:

> Well, that's really cool. I think that's great that there's equal participation. But for me, like, in my opinion, I think it starts when you get into high school. . . . My teammates have probably heard me complain how the boys' basketball games get so many more fans, yet we could argue that we're better than them in our performance. And there's always this thing that women's basketball teams need to be like the top, that elite, to get fans, and a boys' basketball team can just be a team that's average or below average, and they get fans.
>
> Even in high school, I had Paige Bueckers on my team, but prior to her junior, senior year when we actually started getting fans, there was no one ever at our games. And even then, you could say Hopkins was an amazing team at that time, but people were like, "You guys are too good. I don't want to go watch a blowout." Whereas, like, if our boys' team was too good, they would still go watch blowouts. So I think when it just comes to fans, women have to work twice as hard. Or just be at a certain level to receive that support.

Matching Whalen's gray-and-black fleece, black pants, and white Nikes was a member of her coaching staff, and another coach who could be identified by name, face, and her place in the rafters: Rachel Banham.

Banham's pro career hasn't followed the same storybook as her college years. She struggled to get minutes early on with the Sun as a

young player. Her rookie season was cut short by a knee injury requir-
ing microfracture surgery. In year two, she came back to Minnesota
as a visiting player and played just 3:03. Banham told me:

> Yeah, it's hard, especially when you're coming home and
> you have your entire family and friends and fan base and
> all that here. It's hard and I couldn't control it, but it was
> just hard not to have some of the opportunities, not even to
> just get better and get the experience. You know, I wasn't
> expecting a lot of minutes. But just getting the experience,
> especially at that young age, when you're just trying to learn
> the system, learn the league.
>
> I remember kind of feeling sad, but I wasn't like crying
> or anything, and I just remember feeling kind of sad. But
> I just was telling myself, "Look at everybody who's here to
> support you." And I was just trying to remember the posi-
> tives of it.

Banham played four years in Connecticut, but she firmly believed
she had more to give the game. Finally, that chance came along with
coming back home to Minnesota on February 25, 2020. She relished
the opportunity, not only to play more regularly for Cheryl Reeve, who
talked to her about her role, but in front of her friends and family.

Of course, then COVID happened, and her "homecoming" that
first year was in Florida with the Wubble. By the end of 2023, though,
she's finished her fourth season with the Lynx, playing critical minutes
as both a point guard and a deadly shooter off the bench. In her first
115 games and nearly 1,750 minutes with the Lynx, she's shooting
39.1 percent from three, with an assist percentage of 21.6. She's doing

it in smaller bursts, but it's very easy to see the Rachel Banham she's always been when she gets time on the floor. "That's why sometimes you find a home," Banham said. "Like in Connecticut, I didn't really get to play, and there's plenty of reasons, but then I got to come to Minnesota, and I've kind of found myself."

And she's even getting to help that next generation directly. She and Lindsay had been texting throughout her time coming up through Minnesota's system, though the friendship matured, Banham said, as she got to the pros. So when Lindsay needed a director of quality control on her staff, and Cheryl told her Rachel would be great, it was a perfect fit. Of her coaching fit, Rachel said:

> I think, being a point guard, you just communicate a lot. And I love to talk—so that came really naturally, because coaching, you have to be able to communicate effectively. . . . And also you're dealing with so many different things when you're the point guard, and you have to know so many different things. Your brain is just filled with so much information because I need to know what the five needs to be doing, what the two's doing, and also what I'm doing—so I feel like that translates so well to coaching . . . all that, it does come naturally when you've played point guard and then you transition to being a coach. You just kind of have it.

But the growth of the game makes success ever harder. A talented group of young players showed plenty of flashes of brilliance, but the Gophers finished 2022–23 just 11–19, 4–14 in the Big Ten. Many observers believed Lindsay Whalen, who had given so much to the U, who had produced another stellar recruiting class to support her four rising sophomores, should have been given more time. It was hard not to compare her record to that of Cheryl Littlejohn, whose job was safe until she was investigated, found to have committed multiple violations, and asked players to lie for her during the investigation, according to the final report. Winning just one Big Ten game, getting blown out by Indiana in the first round of the Big Ten Tournament, wasn't going to get her fired. But even with a team that never gave up, that played Penn State close, came back late, won four Big Ten games, and was getting Nia Holloway back healthy as well—Whalen wasn't given a chance to see that through forced to resign by Minnesota AD Mark Coyle in March 2023.

Braun told me in May 2023:

> The last game in the locker room and even postgame interviews, the way we were talking to each other, it's like, "We're not finished yet." Like, this is just the beginning. There wasn't any part of any of us that thought it was going to be the end, you know, for that whole staff and everything. So it was definitely a big shock to us.
>
> We found out the next day, actually. They told us to come in. So it just all was a really quick turnaround, and obviously a lot of emotions. And we thought with maybe one more year, we could have helped turn it around. And it could have been looking up from there. But I guess . . . like I said, some things . . . just happen. And we've got to move on and move forward.

Lindsay Whalen was the victim of her own success in this way. She'd proven what Minnesota could be, and in the eyes of many, even some who should have known better, should be. The underlying factors to make that true—that investment and other inputs are necessary to success, rather than simply picking a talented coach and hoping for the best—were ignored.

The four rising sophomores stayed, however. Braun said each of the four of them gave one another space to make their own decisions. But they came independently to the belief that they could build something lasting at Minnesota together. Braun said:

> I put it on social media as early as I did because I was just kind of sick of people making assumptions and saying, "Oh, gosh, there's no way she stays." I'm loyal to Minnesota. I'm from here. I love Minnesota, and I want to do it for the university and for the people that are from here. And I just think that, that shows a lot to younger kids, to younger generations, if you want to keep, you know, in-state talent, that it can be done. And you've just got to stay loyal, and believe through the process. And that was kind of my takeaway, and that's what I led with, to be able to stay, and I'm just super happy, super glad, I made this decision.

The Lynx too, as of this writing, are the victim of their own success, not getting to pick in the lottery after their 2010 selection of Moore until 2023, when they finally took advantage of missing the playoffs and selected Diamond Miller second overall, a New Jersey product who displays a combination of will and athleticism that fits well with what Cheryl Reeve looks for in her players.

Reeve also made the decision to stay after the 2022 season. She was a free agent, and her old friend and rival Lin Dunn is the general manager of the Indiana Fever. Dunn flew her to Indiana, trying to get her to start again, to take over a team that was about to add the best player in college basketball, Aliyah Boston, to their roster with the top overall pick in the 2023 draft. Cheryl and Carley had come a long way from seeing their teams fold. Now multiple WNBA teams had the wherewithal to fight over Cheryl. Reeve signed a five-year deal. Ollie gets to stay in the same school, with the same friends. And Ollie's grandfather, who never got to meet him, or see his daughter become this generation's most important basketball figure, would be so proud of the stability and lucrative opportunities his daughter has found in the game she loves so much.

But the build, this time, will be slower. The Lynx built a best-in-class practice facility back in 2015. Now the Las Vegas Aces and New York Liberty and Seattle Storm are doing the same, with more teams expected to follow. Breanna Stewart was a free agent following the 2022 season, and even met with the Lynx, perhaps as a courtesy to Reeve, now her head coach with USA Basketball as well. But Stewart didn't have to choose between playing close to her home in Syracuse, New York, and playing for a team that co-brands its NBA and WNBA franchises at every opportunity, and invests in the well-being of its players. Teams across the league are copying the Minnesota Lynx playbook. It doesn't mean Cheryl won't build again. It just means there's more competition to do so, that it will require a new way forward. It's growth of the game, writ large, and Cheryl wouldn't have it any other way.

That night in November, Peps found that break in the action and began running up and down the sideline, waving her Gophers blanket as she flew across the sideline, the crowd rising to cheer her, the pep band coming alive for it, drawing a grin from Banham along the sideline. Peps and Vicky finished their summer on the carnival circuit. Then it was Minnesota basketball season once more—time for them to enjoy the development of Braun, Holloway, Battle, and Heyer at Williams Arena. And on November 19, Paige Bueckers and the UConn Huskies came to town.

Here in 2023, women who want to play at the highest level don't have to go anywhere but can go everywhere. Braun, who finished the season with Minnesota, went and played for USA Basketball's 3x3 team at the Nations League Final in the summer of 2023, drew the attention of WNBA front offices, and then flew back home in time to catch a Lynx game ahead of preparing for a Gophers season under a new head coach Dawn Plitzuweit. Peps and Vicky love the way the group is playing defense for Coach P. As 2024 began, they had high hopes for the future of the program, for basketball in Minnesota, and for the stars who would learn from Mara Braun as surely as she learned from those who came before her.

"People are starting to realize that women's basketball is the real deal and that it's really good basketball," Braun told me. "Of course, things aren't always going to be exactly how we want [them], but I just think the ongoing awareness and just understanding of women's basketball, where it's been and how far it's come—it's not at the point where we want it to be, and it may never be, but just how far we've come is pretty dang cool."

ACKNOWLEDGMENTS

THIS BOOK HAS been gestating over the past five years, in idle conversations, long interviews, obscure connections, and vital history I was determined to document. It would not exist without the help of everyone listed here and many people who aren't.

My biggest thanks to everyone who so generously gave of their time and memories, particularly Peps Neuman and Vicky Nelson, Cheryl Reeve, Carley Knox, Lindsay Whalen, Rachel Banham, Maya Moore, Seimone Augustus, Sylvia Fowles, Mara Braun, Nia Holloway, Mallory Heyer, Amaya Battle, Paige Bueckers, Caitlin Clark, Lisa Bluder, and so many others. If nothing more comes from this book than a greater understanding of how much Peps and Vicky matter, it will be a success in my eyes.

Huge shout-out to Trenten Gauthier for not only helping to arrange interviews in Minnesota but even driving me to them.

Thank you to John Molina for introducing me to Peps, Vicky, and so many other early legends of the game, both through your work and direct introductions.

Thank you to my editor Jeff Fedotin and the team at Triumph Books for making me sound smarter; to Noah Amstadter and everyone at Triumph for believing in my vision for this book; and to publicist extraordinaire Stefani Szenda for selling me to the masses.

Thank you to Mel Greenberg, Kent Youngblood, and the scores of other journalists who covered generations of women's basketball players, ensuring both a record of what they accomplished and a trail to pursue as I sought to tell these stories with the added benefit of hindsight.

Thank you to everyone I work with at *The* Next Women's Basketball Newsroom (thenexthoops.com) and the *IX Women's Sports Newsletter* (theixsports.com) for helping tell these stories fully today and tomorrow, and specifically Alex Simon, Kathleen Gier, and Jenn Hatfield for covering for me while I reached the final stages of writing this book and reminding me to prioritize my health too.

Thank you to my in-laws, Hilary and Jason Schwartz, for not only watching my children as I made so many work trips but fiercely advocating for my work everywhere they go.

As ever, this book is only possible because I have the belief in myself and vision to pursue a path previously unseen from my mom, Myrna Megdal, and the relentless work ethic to see it through to its conclusion from my dad, Ira Megdal. I hope this book makes you proud. I am certain you'll tell me, and in my mom's case, tell everyone she meets, too.

Forever: none of this matters without the chance to share it with the love of my life, Rachel, and the sources of purest joy in my life, Mirabelle and Juliet.

To every young woman shooting hoops by herself against a barn, or in a city park, or just in her dreams at bedtime: Everything is possible. And you can make it happen. As Peps always puts it: "Think women's basketball."

SOURCES

Interviews:

Seimone Augustus

Geno Auriemma

Rachel Banham

Amaya Battle

Sue Bird

Lisa Bluder

Mara Braun

Paige Bueckers

Caitlin Clark

Monika Czinano

Anne Donovan

Ann Meyers Drysdale

Lin Dunn

Clare Duwelius

Sylvia Fowles

Kim Franchi

Mallory Heyer

Nia Holloway

Molly Bolin Kazmer

Carley Knox

Karen Healey Lange

Renee Montgomery

Maya Moore

Vicky Nelson

Elvera "Peps" Neuman

Mandy Pearson

Cheryl Reeve

Katie Smith

Lindsay Whalen

Books:

Irons, Maya Moore. *Love and Justice: A Story of Triumph on Two Different Courts.* New York: Andscape Books, 2023.

Molina, John. *Barnstorming America: Stories from the Pioneers of Women's Basketball.* Sikeston, MO: Acclaim Press, 2016.

Articles:

Wilson, Kristen. "A Place for Women: University Gymnasiums, 1867–1969." *Iron Game History*, 16, no. 1 (Winter 2021): 54–62., https://starkcenter.org/igh /igh-v16/igh-v16-n1/igh1601p54.pdf.

Newspapers and Newsletters:

Berkeley Gazette

Berkshire Eagle

Bismarck Tribune

Deseret News

Detroit Free Press

Glens Falls Post Star

Indianapolis Star

Ionia Sentinel-Standard

Knoxville News-Sentinel

Lima Morning Star and Republican-Gazette

Mamaroneck Daily Times

Minnesota-Morris Alumni Newsletter

Reno Journal-Gazette

San Francisco Call

St. Cloud Times

Washington Post

Websites:

125.Stanford.edu

Acrossthetimeline.com

APBR.org

ASAPsports.com

Audacy.com/KYWNewsRadio

Bentleyfalcons.com

Blackfives.org

Calbearshistory.com ("The World's First Women's College Basketball Team")

ESPN.com

GoExplorers.com

Gophersports.com   Obamawhitehouse.archives.gov
Minnpost.com   Stathead.com
MLive.com   Theplayerstribune.com
NCAA.com   WNBA.com
NJ.com

Other Sources:

Knox, Carley. "Behind Closed Locker Room Doors: How Homophobia Operates
in Collegiate Division I Women's Athletics." Graduate thesis for master's in
education, Bowling Green State University, 2004.
Solinger, Jayne. "Daughters of the Game." Minnesota Public Radio, November 29,
2005, radio broadcast.
Vella, Emilia "On Your Mark, Get Set, Gender! The Politicality of Women in
Sports." Senior project, Bard College, 2023.